WHEN WE WERE ONE

Also by W. C. Heinz

The Professional

The Fireside Book of Boxing
  editor

The Surgeon

Run to Daylight!
  with Vince Lombardi

MASH
  with H. Richard Hornberger, M.D.

Emergency

Once They Heard the Cheers

American Mirror

The Book of Boxing
  coeditor with Nathan Ward

What a Time It Was
  The Best of W. C. Heinz on Sports

WHEN WE WERE ONE

Stories of World War II

W. C. Heinz

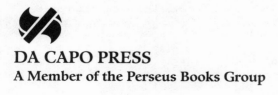

DA CAPO PRESS
A Member of the Perseus Books Group

Designed by Reginald Thompson
Set in 11-point Janson by the Perseus Books Group

Cataloging-in-Publication data for this book is available from the Library of Congress.

First Da Capo Press edition 2002
First Da Capo Press paperback edition 2003
ISBN 0–306–81208–8

Published by Da Capo Press
A Member of the Perseus Books Group
http://www.dacapopress.com

Da Capo Press books are available at special discounts for bulk purchases in the U.S. by corporations, institutions, and other organizations. For more information, please contact the Special Markets Department at the Perseus Books Group, 11 Cambridge Center, Cambridge, MA 02142, or call (800) 255-1514 or (617) 252-5298, or e-mail j.mccrary@perseusbooks.com.

1 2 3 4 5 6 7 8 9—06 05 04 03

The civilian combat correspondent implanted on a war front, whether on land or at sea, is a camp follower. For transportation, food, lodging, and any amenities, he or she is expected, in turn, to provide the service that links the war front to the home front.

Certainly that was true of the coverage of World War II in the European theater where, at worst, the shelter of ruined cities and towns was usually available, as was not always so in the Pacific and Far East theaters. If the correspondent was of draft age, as was this one, and he accepted that his own career as a journalist was being advanced while those of his peers, his protectors, were on hold, some forever, he knew for the rest of his life he would be in debt.

It is to those who, in all this country's wars, fought for us and died in the doing, whether on this earth or in its skies, that this book, in all humility and with the utmost gratitude, is dedicated.

CONTENTS

DISPATCHES FROM
THE *NEW YORK SUN*
(1945)

NIGHT ATTACK
(A six-part series)

"THE MORNING THEY SHOT THE SPIES" AND OTHER FEATURES
(After the War)

DISPATCHES

FROM THE *NEW YORK SUN* (1944)

Sun Reporter on U.S. Battleship Tells How Navy Fought on D-Day

ABOARD A UNITED STATES BATTLESHIP[1] OFF THE COAST OF FRANCE, JUNE 6 (DELAYED).—On the bridge men shivered and peered into the inky blackness ahead, and in a square, white, box-like room one level below the superstructure, others stood with phones to their ears, and still another, sweating, bent over parallel rulers and charts—and that's how $90,000,000 worth of your battleship moved along a channel swept virtually clear of German mine fields in the dark hours before dawn of invasion day.

High up in the foremast and at stations all over the ship, lookouts held their glasses to their eyes. *Somewhere out there ahead the small green light of a floating buoy bobbed, and on the bridge Captain Powell M. Rhea, of Fayetteville, Arkansas, bent down to the speaking tube before him.*[2]

---

[1]U.S.S. *Nevada*
[2]Parts of this article were cut by U.S. military censors and didn't appear in the published version. That material appears in italics.

"We're coming to one-nine-seven, Baker. Can we ease her around a little now?"

Beneath, in that white, box-like chartroom, Commander Robert Baker, of Colorado Springs, bent over a waist-high chart-covered table lit by a yellow neon light, and placed the sharp point of a yellow wooden pencil at the intersection of two lines. Then he turned to the voice tube at his left.

"No, sir. You've got to wait for a second red buoy," he said, *and then he turned to one of the sailors with earphones on his head and a phone on his chest and said: "and tell Info when this buoy is abeam to get me the bearing on the next one."*

Seaman Second Class Ernest Shandelmayer, of Mechanicsburg, Pennsylvania, repeated the message into the phone. While he spoke another sailor came in and took off his steel helmet and spoke out of the corner of his mouth: "They just got another of our planes. A great big flash, and that's all ya see."

"Believe me," Commander Baker said, "we're not at any damn picnic now. All I've got to be glad for is those minesweepers. Those minesweepers have done a damn fine job, and I mean that. Now get me a sounding."

Quartermaster Third Class Roger Bell, of Chicago, walked over and snapped the switch on the gray dial-fronted cabinet. He reported the depth of 28 fathoms when the voice came over the inter-ship radio: "To all ships astern. *Texas*[3] has mine on her port bow. Repeat: *Texas* has mine on her port bow."

Suddenly now no one spoke. The great ship now was as silent in the great silence as she was black in the great blackness as she felt her way slowly forward.

"Will one of you lads pour me a cup of coffee?" Commander Baker said, turning from the table. "And put in about a teaspoon of sugar and a fair portion of cream."

---

[3]U.S.S. *Texas*

Then he turned back and bent over the table again, and the yellow light above shone on his back. Bell, who had mixed the coffee, handed it to him and he sipped it slowly for it was hot.

"Baker," came the voice of the captain over the tube, "we seem to have lost our buoys."

"Yes, sir," Baker said.

"What do you suggest?"

"Stand on."

"In other words, you're gonna lead us in without buoys?"

"Yes, sir."

"Does that mean this hasn't been swept?"

"Yes, sir."

"Then the ship is yours."

"Yes, sir," Baker said, bending back over the table again. "And damn this helmet. Travis said he'd fix it for me and now it's always falling over my eyes."

So the commander took off his helmet and put it out of the way on the chart table, and still no one spoke. Over the table the commander moved his parallel rulers and on the chart he made small marks and the sailors in the room with him were silent as they watched and waited even as men elsewhere were silent too as they too waited.

"Come to two one five," he said.

"Two one five," the captain's voice said from the tube.

"Now come to two oh five."

"Two oh five," the captain said, and then there was a long pause and he said: "Say, Baker, there's a green buoy forty degrees on port."

"Good," Baker said. "You can drop the hook anytime now, sir. We're there. The ship is yours."

"Thank you, Baker."

Outside the dark stillness of the Bay of the Seine was no longer silent, for there was a great deep scraping as over the forecastle slid the great chain and ten tons of anchor found its bed in the sands off the shore of France.

"Those minesweepers," Baker said, "have one tough racket. For my money, they're okay."

At this point we saw and heard everything flyable in England roar overhead and plant their loads in Hitler's front yard. The parachute flares and flak were like Coney Island on the Fourth of July, but the huge pillars of orange flame and black smoke were like nothing else on this earth.

Concussion Shook Battleship

Even at this distance, this ship shook with the concussion from the falling bombs, and the smoke and dust filled the eyes of the watchers. Yet the scene was one of strange beauty as billowing gray smoke formed graceful patterns against the sunset hues—strange beauty that was interrupted by the sight of returning planes breaking from their formations and plummeting toward the sea in flames.

Later, with the rest of this bombardment group, we moved in a long, silent line again to anchor here and await a dawn that seemed to come more reluctantly than any dawn that these men have ever known. With the first streaks of the dawn of D-Day lighting the east, the first of the long line of amphibious assault craft moved up on the starboard beam like black boxes on an endless white string.

Three minutes later, with a great whining overhead, the first shell fired toward us landed in a great cloud of smoke and spray off the port bow. On the bridge, Captain Powell M. Rhea of Fayetteville, Arkansas, took the first bite of a doughnut and the first sip of his coffee.

Battleship Stands Tight

At 5:32 A.M. all of our destroyers between us and the shore opened up with five-inch guns, and yet our orders were to stand tight. In absolute silence the great ship stood still and overhead the planes droned and everywhere men waited.

Now the sky in the east reddened, and suddenly overhead again was a great whining and the ship shook as if she were a toy, as first one and then a second shell landed off her starboard bow. Quietly, as if asking for a light, Captain Rhea spoke only two words, and suddenly the ship shook again as her 5-inch gun mounts were wreathed in smoke and flame, and one ship's answer was on its way.

Arching upward and seeming to converge as they descended, each mount's shells looked like so many shooting stars until they were lost in the distance and became faraway flashes of flame on the beach.

The Big Guns Speak

For five minutes, then, men in the tight, yellow-painted interiors of the gun turrets bent over lines of blue-painted shells with yellow noses and, straightening up, rammed retribution into brazen breaches. Then, below decks, sitting on a leather-covered soda fountain stool, Fire Controlman Myers saw two yellow lights flash and two white lines meet, and squeezed that index finger.

Back from Grave at Pearl Harbor, U.S.S. *Nevada* Shatters Nazi Line

ABOARD THE U.S.S. *NEVADA* OFF THE COAST OF FRANCE, JUNE 9 (DELAYED).—The man who said they never come back was wrong. He was wrong by the 1,454,722 pounds of steel and T.N.T. that this blackened ghost from a watery grave at Pearl Harbor has hurled in the last three days upon the German beach defenses, the German gun emplacements and the German troops and tank concentrations opposing the American landings in the Bay of Seine area.

As this mighty man-of-war and the rest of the Allied armada steamed brazenly into Hitler's front yard on Tuesday, she was the first to be fired upon from the shore batteries—batteries which moments later she silenced. Since then she has stood here, an angry, defiant monster, remembering a sunny Sunday morning two and a half years ago and halfway around the world, and spitting fire and steel till the paint was burned from her guns and her decks were piled high with empty shell

cases like big brass umbrella holders that tumbled into
the water and, almost submerged, floated away.

Since forty-five minutes before H hour on D-Day,
when in the cold, gray light of dawn she began punch-
ing holes in the concrete seawall for the troops to pour
through, the *Nevada* has taken on between twenty-five
and thirty land batteries, consisting of as many as 125
guns of sizes up to eight inches; two concentrations of
tanks and field artillery plus several large concentrations
of troops, including an infantry assembly point where
the enemy was mustering for a counter-attack; several
convoys of trucks and other motorized transport and
numerous machine gun nests, pill boxes and other sec-
ondary fortifications. In less than twenty minutes yesterday she sent shells arching into a concentration of
ninety tanks and more than twenty lorries in the woods
with such effectiveness that none escaped, observation
reported.

She's Taken It, Too

This *Nevada* has been handing it out with a vengeance,
and yet she has been taking it, too. She has been taking it
not from the enemy but from herself as, hour after hour
through the long days, the concussion from her big guns
has shaken her as if she were a frail, tin toy and not the
32,000-ton steel dreadnought that she is.

When this great ship moved in here last Monday
night, picking her way silently through the darkness
with the cruisers and destroyers in this task force sup-
porting the easternmost American landings, she was but-
toned up tight and ready to go. Beneath her decks, in
water-tight compartments, were all the extra food, dress
blues, china, glassware, library books, tablecloths, office
files, brooms, mirrors and the thousands of other things

that make this huge ship a home for 2,500 people. And at clean, tight battle-stations were clean, eager men.

But that was Monday night, and this is being written at 3 A.M. on Friday. These men have now been at their battle-stations for seventy hours, and neither stations nor men are clean any longer.

These now are men with dirty, unshaven faces, and red, swollen eyes. These are men who have slept for only an hour or two during all this time; slept for fifteen minutes at a time sitting upright in radio rooms, slept for half an hour at a time sprawled over one another on the gun mounts. Yet these men are ready to go again at any minute.

Strain Is Severe

Throughout the ship now, and from her own blows, the paint has peeled from bulkheads, and rivets and bolts have been sprung. Below decks, water connections have been broken and dust and dirt have been shaken down everywhere, and on the main deck are burnt cork from the shell casings, torn cardboard from K rations and burnt silk that would have been in milady's stockings if it had not been used for powder bags.

Actually the *Nevada* started to come back a long time ago. She started back on February 15, 1942, when they pumped her out and raised her, blacked and broken, from that sandy beach near the sugar cane field at Pearl Harbor. She had come a long way back in April 1943, when for four days she ran through fog and reefs to Massacre Bay to pump shells into Attu.

One the bridge now stands a man who has been there since 11 P.M. last Saturday, June 3. And he is tired and haggard, but he is still carrying on. He is from Fayetteville, Arkansas. He is Captain Powell M. Rhea.

The *Nevada* Bows
Out with Her Fame
Safe in History

ABOARD U.S.S. *NEVADA*, ENGLISH CHANNEL, JUNE 20.—In their bunks now the men are breathing heavily and in shower stalls there is the sound once again of running water and everywhere there is this music; for this is music with which a great ship, a great ship from a Pearl Harbor grave, is bowing out from the first phase of the invasion of Europe, a phase which it has written with flame and steel its name in the naval annals.

In the dim light of early morning yesterday, long before the first rays of the rising sun had painted with orange the dirt cliffs of Normandy and shattered, broken pillboxes like crushed cardboard containers atop them, this great, gray floating fortress like a tired and massive warrior, its back turned on scenes of destruction it had wrought, bowed from the Bay of the Seine. It bowed out because the Army it helped ashore in the early light of another morning almost two weeks ago, had now grown from the shelter of its flaming decks.

When she bowed out, however, this ship bowed out in glory. On the shores of France now are men who will never forget her name and in the port towns of England small boatmen know of her fame for men who saw what she did will remember always.

What these men saw was the *Nevada* blanketed in sheets of flame, her own steel tearing holes in Hitler's west wall, holes so big an army could drive tanks right through. What these men saw was the *Nevada* wreathed in clouds of her own amber smoke uprooting gun emplacements, scattering pillboxes and smashing tank and troop concentrations, but what you, as the only newspaperman aboard this American battleship in this invasion, saw was men rather than a machine that did all of this.

Willing to Ground Ship

You saw men like Captain Powell M. Rhea of Fayetteville, Arkansas, and Commander Howard A. Yeager of Salina, Kansas, when ordered to accomplish certain objectives, resolve to run this ship ashore and turn her into a fort if necessary. You saw men of the gunnery department from Lieutenant Commander Charles W. Travis of Murfreesboro, Tennessee, the gun boss, to seaman, first class, Charles J. Gibson of Lees Summit, Missouri, who, until relieved, in the first two hours and ten minutes of the invasion loaded 26,730 pounds, or more than thirty tons, of 5-inch shells with fingers of the right hand broken.

You saw these men and hundreds of others who, in engine room and repair parties and lookout posts, stood at stations for seventy-nine hours at a stretch and now you would like to give the total sum of what they did.

In the six days in which they actually fired with the $90,000,000 weapon you placed in their hands they hurled over four dozen targets 1,792,574 pounds of steel and explosives. They fired in all from the main battery 1,216 fourteen-inch shells and that is, in all, almost 900 tons and approximately $1,500,000 of your War Bonds that couldn't be better spent.

Between the hours of 9:29 and 11:18 P.M. on D-Day, for example, they sent eighteen 1,200-pound shells screaming for tank and artillery concentrations, eighteen more into troop concentrations and another eighteen in another tank and artillery grouping and fourteen more into an enemy assembly point. On each of these targets shore fire control parties reported, "fire very effective" and, finally, "counter attack destroyed." The next day came congratulations, "information that your missions last night were much valued and beautifully executed."

Nazis Leave Hurriedly

In twenty-one minutes on the night of June 11, they pumped nine 1,200-pounders into enemy artillery batteries and again the next day came congratulations, "your firing last night, first salvo a direct hit on gun. Your fire for effect completely wiped out battery. If all personnel were not killed they left immediately. We have not heard from them since." And that's the way it went.

You could, in fact, cite targets and the results of this pin point precision firing of the ships that the Japs called dead two and one-half years ago, for paragraph after paragraph. You could recite in detail how in another sixty minutes this ship destroyed, on the morning of June 12, a battery of six-inch guns and battery headquarters of the enemy. But it is not of such things that these men are talking now.

In their bunks now the men are breathing heavily, and in shower stalls there is the sound once again of running water, for this is the music with which the great ship bows out, and over all, too, there is lightness in their hearts; lightness held under for many days. In the ward room now Lieutenant (j.g.) Eugene J. Conant of Detroit kids about the days when as a diver he helped raise the *Nevada* from the mud at Pearl Harbor. In the crew's quarters a sailor brags now how Lieutenant Commander H. Todd Stradford of 333 East 43d Street, Manhattan, took his appendix out during the firing in the Bay of the Seine. Elsewhere the men were reading mail a destroyer brought alongside yesterday.

Names Daughter for Target

Lieutenant (j.g.) Edward J. O'Brien of Quincy, Massachusetts, reads over again that his daughter Caren was born on June 8. That is a name picked long before Carentan, one of the major objectives, and yet Lieutenant Commander Philip F. Ashler Jr. of 1645 Putnam Avenue, Ridgewood, Queens, has been handed the biggest laugh of all.

All during the battle of the Bay of the Seine Commander Ashler stood on the bridge and broadcast by public address system to men below on decks his eyewitness account and now he has received this form letter in the mail: "Dear Subscriber: I am sending you this issue of *Time* Magazine by air mail because it carries the story of the invasion. I hope it will help give you the picture of this great day in the war—."

Battleships are still queen of the seas.

Following her performance in the Bay of the Seine, the Nevada *and others of that bombardment group moved west on June 25 to drop anchor off Cherbourg and pound shore batteries and inland targets in support of the liberation of the first French port. On August 14 she was off the southern French coast, backing those landings and again firing inland. Certainly she will go down in the history of this country's naval warfare, but she went down in fact when scuttled by American hands on November 1, 1952. Now what is left of her is left for the fishes, for her remains lie at the bottom of Eniwetok Atoll in the Pacific where, as part of a fleet of diverse vessels, she was submitted to the world's first hydrogen bomb test. The coup de grace came from a sub-launched torpedo.*

w.c.h., 2002

A Ride to Mons
in Moonlight

MONS, BELGIUM, SEPT. 4 (DELAYED).—You meet a lot of people in covering a war, and some of them you remember and some of them you forget. But no matter how long you live, you'll always remember the major who took you to Mons.

It was Saturday night. It was just about six hours after you had crossed the Belgian border with the main column of American armor, and the unit you were with had bivouacked about five miles from Mons while some tanks had gone on to claim the city.

You hadn't gone on because you had come a long way that day and you were dusty and tired. Besides that you had found a house where there was an extra double bed with clean sheets and where the people were celebrating their liberation and had asked you to stay. So Mons could wait.

This was going to be rather wonderful, you thought, because you had raced so to catch up that you had come away without any bedroll, and besides, sheets are one of those luxuries you live for in war. It was while you were talking about those sheets and how wonderful they were going to be that you met the major, who said he hadn't slept between sheets in what seemed like years.

So you invited him to sleep with you, and he accepted.

Celebration in Mons

The major and you had gone to the house and had gotten a jug of water. You both had washed and shaved by flashlight, and then you had gone again to the command post to see what the word was from up ahead. It was after you had been there a while that the report came through that the tanks had reached Mons and that there was quite a celebration in the city.

And then you decided that it might be quite a story at that, being in Mons with the first American troops to enter the first Belgian city.

It was a nice thing for the major, you know now, to offer to take you to Mons. He had just said that if you wanted to go to Mons he'd take you. And so you sat around and talked a while about the chances of getting there, and the major was frank about that, too.

The major explained that our tanks were in Mons but that he couldn't say what the road would be like up to Mons. He said there were undoubtedly Germans on both sides of the road who had been passed by our tanks. He admitted that the moon was bright, but he said that if you wanted to go, he'd take you.

Knew He'd Get You There

And somehow you knew he would, because you knew he was the kind of a guy who would do anything he wanted, even in war.

He was a soft-spoken guy, this major, but he was the kind of a guy you knew you were safe with, no matter

where he took you. He was out of the Carolinas somewhere and he was a young, lean, hard, good-looking guy
with blue eyes and a soft voice and that air of being able
to do anything he wanted.

So you decided you'd go to Mons. You got into the
jeep and you went to Mons. It was a ride that you'll always remember, just as you'll always remember the major.

When you started, the major put his carbine between
the seats, but he didn't say anything, and then you were
out on the road. It was one of those wonderful silver
nights; the moon was almost full and there was a light
breeze, and on either side of the road the poplars were
singing like they sing in the States.

Confidence in Major

And although there were dark patches of woods here and
there along the sides you didn't worry because you knew
that the major was the kind of a guy with whom you
could go anywhere.

Well, when you got to Mons there wasn't anything.
The tanks were on both sides of the city and in the town
there was nothing. There were no people and there was
no sound, just shadows and moonlight against the stone
fronts of the houses. And so after you had ridden slowly
through this for ten minutes you started back.

On the way back you talked about many things. You
talked about the moon, which the major said was a Carolina moon. You said it was a Vermont moon, and then
you talked about how wonderful it was going to be to
sleep between sheets.

On the way you passed dark woods, but you knew
nothing would happen because you felt that with the
major you could go anywhere.

Colonel Sends for Major

It was a wonderful ride in the cool silver quiet, that
night, and when you drove into the camp it seemed a
shame that it was over. You had just parked the jeep and
were covering it over with branches when a G.I. said
that the colonel wanted to see the major.

"Don't wait for me," the major said. "You hit those
sheets, and be sure to leave just room enough for me,
'cause, boy, I'm tired."

Then the major walked away after the G.I. and you
went into the house and got in bed, and it seems now
that you fell right to sleep. When you awakened it was
after 6 o'clock and you could hear the motors turning
over outside. At first you forgot all about the major and
then you saw his shaving set and toothbrush, and you
felt kind of funny, although you kept telling yourself it
was silly because the major wasn't that kind of a guy.

When you went over to the command post one of the
captains told you about it. He said that the major and
one of the lieutenants had had to go back to Mons.
When they hadn't come back in the morning they had
sent a sergeant up the road and he had found the jeep by
the side of the road where it had been sprayed by bullets,
and then he had found the bodies of the major and the
lieutenant in a ditch nearby.

So you went back to the room and got the major's
things together and gave them to the chaplain. And even
now you can't believe it. You see, you'll always remember this major who took you to Mons as the kind of a
guy who could do anything he wanted—even in war.

Harried Germans
Don't Have Time
Even to Bury Their Dead

WITH THE UNITED STATES FIRST ARMY IN GERMANY, SEPT. 19.—In a dark, pine forest in the middle of the Siegfried Line they are totaling up for Germany today the price of two wars. They are carrying out, these Americans, what might be but a simple problem in addition, this process of adding to the fathers of '14 their sons of '44.

This is a beautiful forest here, this Rhineland forest where the Siegfried Line is behind and beyond. It is one of those dark cathedral places where the pines are old and straight and all stand in aisles.

This is a different war from that other war. It is a war in which it is the Americans who are adding here the German sons to the German fathers, because there was no time for the Germans.

When you came today to this German cemetery in the middle of this German forest you were stopped by the whiteness of the stucco beneath the dark green of the trees and against the blackness under them. It was a

Spanish place, with porticos and rounded arches, and when you drove to it a white rabbit ran across in front of the jeep and the driver stopped to let it pass, because even in war men slow down to let a rabbit pass although overhead the shells scream on.

Occupied by Infantrymen

Against the walls of this white stucco place was the green of formal shrubbery and under the porticos were Americans with rifles over their shoulders or carrying them in their hands. This was an infantry company and it was they who told you that this was the German cemetery they moved into the night before.

So you walked along the portico and went inside and there you saw what the Germans had no time for in this war, when they move so fast.

On the gray stone floor, in front, were potted shrubs and behind them were fifteen brown wooden caskets. These were German sons the Germans had not had time to add to the German fathers.

How long these German sons had lain there in their brown wooden caskets you did not know, but it must have been several days. On all the caskets there were fastened with thumb tacks white cards on which were written the names in the same German script and on one was a dying spray of red and white dahlias tied with white ribbon on which German letters said, "To Our Comrade, a Last Greeting."

When you walked from the room you walked along a corridor and there were many doors. When you looked in one there were two Germans lying on litters made of branches of trees and wooden slats from boxes and there were gray German blankets over the faces, just as there were also over the faces of the Germans lying on the gray stone floor of the portico, because the Germans had not had time.

So when you stepped off the portico and walked along the crushed-stone path, you left the sons behind. Where the path led, their fathers had gone a long time before.

Dates of First World War

On each side of the path were small evergreens and laurel leaves, shiny because they were damp, and when it came to the fathers it was not hard to tell that they had gone along this path a long time before. On these stones, amid shrubs, were dates—1914, 1916, 1918—but you did not have to look at the dates, for the gray granite of the stones had in some places become black and in others green.

On all these graves was ivy and on some were pots of begonias. On a few were bouquets of gladiolas, asters and zinnias that were beginning to dry now. And overhead, above the towering pines, shells kept whining, for this was still the front line.

You remember that there was one stone in which had been set an oval porcelain plate on which had been reproduced in brown the uniformed figure of this father of 1916. You remember that there was another on which part of the lettering was old and part new, because from North Africa on April 12, 1943, they brought back the son that they might add him to his father.

For fifteen minutes you walked among these graves of the fathers while shells whined overhead and then you turned back and where the fathers' graves ended there was something else. It was an ivy-covered grave in front of a granite pillar among the trees. On the pillar was cut out the figure of a man carrying in one hand a flag. The sleeves of the man's shirt were rolled up and on the right arm was a swastika armband and on the flag held in the left hand was the swastika sign, too.

This Marked a Brownshirt

This was not a father, this man, and he was not a son. This was a Brownshirt who died in one of those abortive putsches in the early thirties and so it was not strange that you should find him here where fathers ended and sons began.

And so that is how in this dark pine forest in the middle of the Siegfried Line, with shells still whining overhead, the Americans find themselves with a strange task. To them has fallen the problem of adding to the fathers of '14 the sons of '44 and of totaling up for Germany the price of two wars.

Bitter Armored Battle
for Stolberg

WITH AN AMERICAN ARMORED DIVISION[1] ON THE OUT-
SKIRTS OF STOLBERG, GERMANY, SEPT. 20.—There were
days after St. Lo and after the Jerries started high-tailing
it beyond the Seine and through Belgium on which this
armor used to reel off thirty or more miles a day and liberate half a dozen towns in one afternoon. In a couple of
hours yesterday afternoon you watched these same boys,
who not so long ago were being pelted with flowers and
smothered with kisses and who kept asking you if the
war was over, make a hundred yards—and it was a long
way.

This is tough terrain here, just west of where Stolberg,
with its sooty factories and their tall, red brick and gray
stone chimneys, sits upon a kind of ridge. You cannot
even walk in anything like a straight line in getting up
near that ridge, because every five or six feet there are
hummocks half as big as a house and everything is covered with bushes and scrub trees. Yet when you caught
up with them the tanks were grinding and lurching, and
stopping, and lurching again.

---

[1] 3rd American Armored Division

Two of those tanks, in fact, had made the top ridge, and were just about 200 yards from the first three stone houses on the edge of the town. Running low from hummock to hummock, Indian fashion, the infantry was beginning to fill in after them now. Behind the hummock where you had flopped, the colonel was just wondering why the Jerries had let the tanks get that far when, above the chatter of the machine guns, came two loud crumps. When you got up enough courage to raise your head, you couldn't see the leading tank at first, and then you saw one of its treads sticking up, because the 88s had hit and somehow it had fallen over.

Meets Perspiring Yank

You do not know what happened on the other side of the tank because, frankly, you just didn't feel like going around to see. After a couple of minutes, lying there in the warm sun and listening to some of our big stuff trying to find that German gun, a G.I. came half-running, half-rolling over the top of a hummock and slid down next to you. He was a good-looking kid, and his face was brown from the sun and clear beads of sweat were dropping from the point of his nose. He was such a nice looking kid you asked him what his name was. He said he was Corporal Henry Hergenrader of Lincoln, Nebraska, and when you asked him about the tank he said they "got out two guys who were in kind of a bad way."

Joined By Another

While you were lying there talking with Hergenrader another G.I. came over the hummock, squatted down about five feet away, put his carbine down on the grass, and ran a hand over his forehead.

"Well," he said after a while, "one of them is out of it for good."

"That was Monithis," he added.

Hergenrader didn't say anything, but just nodded. Then the other G.I., who, you learned later, was Staff Sergeant William Petersimes, of Chicago, asked Hergenrader if they had sent for the medics. Hergenrader said they had, but he guessed maybe the medics couldn't get up, because that was about ten minutes ago.

"Hell, we could have those guys back there by now," said Sergeant Petersimes.

Prepare for Rescue

So the sergeant and the corporal put their carbines down on the grass on the side of the hummock, and then they went over to a pile of German clothes, knapsacks and boots, headed around the bush and pulled off two gray blankets. Then the sergeant bent down and started to run, almost doubled over, and the corporal was right behind him.

It's a wonderful thing the way the American G.I. will accept a situation like that and face it so frankly. Here were two guys without even the protection of the medic's white armbands who were going up with nothing except blankets under their arms to look down the throat of a German anti-tank gun to bring back two other guys whom they didn't even know, except that they knew they were wounded and had to be brought back.

So you were lying there and listening to those machine guns eating away at each other to the left and the heavier stuff whining back and forth and crumping around, and you were trying to bring those two guys back, when you heard the colonel shouting to you to get

the hell over to where he was and that if the Heinies
ever dropped one in this hollow it would be right where
you were.

Runs to Safer Place

You are very much of a dope about such things because
you can never tell where they are coming from except that
they seem to be coming from all sides, so you made a run
to the other side and plopped down and when you did you
almost landed on a G.I. who just kinda rolled away and
said: "This is a hell of a way to make a living isn't it?"

You were no sooner over there it seemed when the
Heinies really opened up. They didn't have the range
with mortars, which were falling everywhere. One shell
fragment cut through a bush right in the middle of the
hollow and another hit the helmet of the G.I. and
bounced about five feet. The G.I. picked it up and
turned it over in his hand and then put it in his pocket.

Right then you thought that the sergeant and the corporal would never get back, but the medics must have
come in another way because you saw two medics, one
carrying the front of each stretcher and the sergeant and
the corporal carrying the backs. When they got into the
hollow they put down the stretchers right in front of you
and under one blanket a guy lay very still and on the
other a tankman kept tossing his head back and forth
and moaning and when one medic pulled the blanket
back you could see that they had made a splint from a rifle and the rifle on the right leg was covered with blood.

Jeep Takes Wounded

You never did know how they got the jeep up there but
they did because pretty soon it came pitching right from

one of the hummocks and with stuff still flying they loaded the two stretchers on the hood of the jeep and climbed in and started half rolling, half riding back.

In a couple of minutes the Heinies kind of paused for breath and so you ducked along the way the jeep had come. Where you walked, crouching between the hummocks, the infantry boys were digging in and some were already in foxholes. In just about two minutes you were back where those tanks had started because it wasn't more than a hundred yards, and yet, because the Heinies were really making a fight for it now here in the last redoubts of the Siegfried Line and it wasn't a parade any more it was a long way.

Still Battle
on Hill Above Aachen

ON DAWSON RIDGE, GERMANY, OCT. 22 (DELAYED).—If you want to go to Aachen now, you can drive in and out at will and there is nothing to stop you, for since Saturday Aachen has been ours. And yet on this ridge the guys who held the key to the city are still dug in—here in the mud and cold and wet and amid the dead, where they have been for thirty-eight days.

This is an ordinary-looking ridge here, this ridge that they have named after a gangling, 31-year-old son of a Texas Baptist pastor. But it happens to be the highest ground in these parts, and so from here you can see Belgium and Holland and just about everything except the way off of this ridge, which is lost in the fog and mist that is Germany.

This ridge is 838 feet high, and 400 yards long in its highest part, and it runs southeast of Verlautenheide toward Stolberg, which are two places that the guys who fought and died here had never heard of before. This ridge had been divided into pasture lots and farming ground, but the sides are torn now and the three red-brick houses are shattered and broken, and only the skeletons of two steel towers still stand at the top, their power lines dangling to the ground.

Here They Stopped 'Em

They have been here for thirty-eight days and thirty-eight nights, these Americans, and the nights have been longer than the days and yet today they tell you that if you go fifty feet farther and show your head over the top of this ridge you will draw fire down upon them all. Besides, there is no need to go any farther because it is here, two miles east of the city, that the gates of Aachen were hinged.

This is where the gates of Aachen were hinged because this is where one forward company—"one lousy little old G Company," as Captain Joseph T. Dawson of Waco, Texas, calls it—stopped the three best divisions that the Germans had to offer. This is where they stopped them with everything from artillery to riflebutts and that other thing that is still called guts, and that is why they never reached the streets of Aachen, these three divisions, and why the gates of the city were hinged here.

They came up on this hillside here, the guys in this G Company, on September 14, and they dug in where you can find them now. They took this hill easily, because then the Germans were still on the run, but the next morning as they looked down they could see the German buildup starting to develop. All day, as they watched from above, they saw the Germans moving up in the woods about 1,000 yards to the northeast, in the orchard to the southeast, and in patches of rough ground in between. And they dug in.

On the morning of the 16th, that German infantry division attacked and when it hit, it hit, as the captain says, "one lousy little old G Company." It hit first with artillery and mortars and then it attacked with at least two companies.

An American Tank Shows Up

"The intensity of the attack carried the enemy into my positions," the captain said, "and I lost men. They weren't wounded. They weren't taken prisoners. They were killed. But we piled them up."

They piled them up, that day, one upon another, as they have piled them up since, for they have taken three major attacks here and there have been very few prisoners. That one lasted from 7 to 11 A.M., and at 1:30 P.M. Lieutenant John D. Burbridge of LaGrange, Georgia, took a platoon and physically drove them back from where the sheer weight of their attack had carried them in.

From then on until October 4, nothing fell on this position here except 500 rounds of artillery a day, from everything from 150's up. And at night it was the same only worse.

"On October 4," the captain said, "that other infantry division hit us. We had had constant shelling for eight hours, and we had had twelve direct hits on what was our command post then, because we were taking it from 270 degrees on the compass. When they stopped coming we could count 350 that we ourselves had killed—not those killed by our artillery or planes, but just by one lousy little old G Company all by itself."

On October 15, an SS Panzer division moved into position below, and struck at 11 o'clock that night. They struck with artillery and they struck with tanks, and behind them came the men, and the first tank that penetrated the position here was an American Sherman that still had the Allied star and insignia of the Fifth Armored Division on it, and had been captured on the Third Army front.

They Die Together

In the darkness of that night, split only by the flash of guns, the spitting of rifles and the cries of men—for the Heinies still holler when they are hit—the gates of Aachen almost swung open here, and for two days they groaned on their hinges.

Those were nights and days when men killed one another with rifle-butts, because it was too close to bring rifles to bear. At one machine-gun position a German toppled dead over the barrel of our gun, and in one foxhole an American fought off death and waited until the German who had shot him came up and looked down upon him, and then the American emptied his Tommy gun in the enemy's face and the two men died, side by side.

Then there was this captain who, they tell you at headquarters, is as good a fighting man as there is in the American Army, and who called for artillery ten yards beyond his own position. But on that 17th of October the gates of Aachen, here on this hillside, were shut for good.

So down in Aachen they have won the city, house to house, and here on this hillside they have won only the right to stay another day, because they are still digging in. In those moments when the artillery shells aren't falling here you can see a G.I. running, bent over low, and under one arm he has a piece of timber and under the other a square of corrugated tin. They tell you that he is improving his position, something that always goes on in these rare moments, because this is where he lives and fights and this is where he doesn't want to die.

Still Hold Key to City

And in piles on the hillside, where they stopped them, the Germans lie. They still lie here because the Germans don't bother with their dead, and when we try to move them, the Germans kill the men who go out to do the job. So they lie here, these Germans, some of them whole and many of them in parts, and the smell is bad.

It is so bad that some guys get sick, but there is one guy in here who, though he was sick when he said it, asked them not to try to move the Germans too far away from the foxholes where he lies day and night.

"Just move the ones that are within ten feet," he said. "I don't think those Krauts have got guts enough to try to come at me if they have to climb over their own dead."

Meanwhile, down in Aachen now, you can drive in and out at will and there is nothing to stop you, for they held the key to the city here, these guys who, if you ask them about it, will tell you that they didn't fight for Aachen, but just to stay on this ridge for another day.

Dawson Holds Line Above Aachen

ON DAWSON RIDGE, GERMANY, OCT. 23 (DELAYED).—
Back at headquarters they'll tell you that Captain
Joseph T. Dawson is as good a fighting man as there is
in the American Army, and they won't be talking about
his D.S.C. or his Purple Heart with clusters, but about
how he led his company first off the beaches in France
and about why they named this ridge here after him.

"I've never seen anything like it before," he was saying. "This is the worst I've ever seen."

The captain is a tall man. He is 6 feet 2, but he is thin
and his clothes fit him loosely, because he has lost
twenty-five pounds over here. His face is bony and he
has large ears and very brown eyes, long straight black
hair and his nose doesn't stick out of his face, but runs
straight along down through the middle.

"Nobody," the captain was saying, "will ever know
what this has been like up here. You aren't big enough to
tell them, and I'm not big enough to tell them, and nobody can tell them."

Candlelight and Maps

This is where they closed the gate to Aachen and where G Company stopped the best that three German divisions had to offer. This just happens to be the highest ridge around here, and when the captain leaned back in a wicker chair he crossed his feet on a wooden table.

In this command post here they had lighted one white candle and one small kerosene lamp, which stood on a table, with maps and magazines around them. On another table against the far wall, dance music was coming from a small shiny radio, and outside in the night would be periods of quiet and periods of great noise.

When there was a period of quiet it was hard to realize that the Germans were 250 yards away. Then there was only this room, and soft dance music coming out from against the wall, and men sitting around straddling chairs, with their arms on the backs of chairs and their chins on their arms; and a small tan dachshund rubbed against your ankles and shoes.

Bullets Cut the Night

"That dog is Freda," the captain said. "She was here when we came up on this hill and she's never gone away."

Then he looked down at the dog and added: "Weren't you, Freda?"

When there was a period of noise you could hear machine guns outside cutting the night in geometric parts, and the whine of our own guns and the crump of theirs.

"Just one lousy little old G Company," the captain said when you had got him to talking about his guys. "Just G.I. privates, corporals, sergeants, and nobody will understand."

The captain said that nobody would understand because you had asked him to tell you about their thirty-
nine nights here. He told you about it right from the
start, the first guy he had had a chance to talk to like that
in thirty-nine days. And now the rifle butts and hand
grenades and the parts of bodies and the screams in the
night were with him again, and he knew that nobody
would understand all that.

"And a kid says, 'I'll take that water to that platoon,'"
he was saying now, and he had taken his feet down and
was leaning forward. "And he starts out. He is about fifty
yards from this doorway and I'm watching him. He is
running fast; then I can see this 88 hit right where he is,
and, in front of my eyes, he is blown apart."

The captain, who is from Waco, Texas, talked for a
long while about things like that. He is a son of a Baptist
pastor and his voice is soft and yet sometimes he uses
strong words.

"What would you do," he said, "if a guy said, 'I can't
take it any more'—just like that? If I lose that man, I lose
a squad. So I grab him by the shirt, and I say: 'You will,
you will. There ain't any going back from this hill except
dead.' And he goes back and he is dead."

The captain was quiet for a moment now, as quiet as
the room, for nobody spoke and there were no guns
barking outside.

"He doesn't know why," he said, "and I don't know
why, and you don't know why. But I have got to answer
to those guys.

'Shut Up!'

"I have got to answer to those guys," he said, and he was
looking right at you, "because I wear bars. I've got the

responsibility and I don't know whether I'm big enough for the job.

"But I can't break now," he was saying and you could see what was going to happen. "I've taken this for thirty-nine days, and I'm in the middle of the Siegfried Line and you want to know what I think? I think it stinks."

And then the captain put his head in his hands and his elbows on his knees, and Captain Joe Dawson, fighting man, sobbed.

There wasn't a sound in the room. You think now that nobody even moved and it must have been for about fifteen seconds. And then suddenly the captain raised his head and did a peculiar thing. Without looking at anybody, he said, "Shut up!"

"Shut up," he said. "I want to hear this. It's the 'Bell Song' from 'Lakme.'"

The radio was clear and the soprano's voice was soft and so was the string music.

"Puccini," somebody said.

"No," the captain said, "not Puccini. Not Puccini, but I can't remember the name of the guy."

Co. G
Holds Ridge,
Key to Aachen

ON DAWSON RIDGE, GERMANY, OCT. 24 (DELAYED).—"G Company," said the captain, "is not anybody. We just got here and somehow we just grasped the idea that we were the old United States Army and we were going to take this place and hold it and that's all."

Captain Joe Dawson, this gangling, 31-year-old son of a Waco, Texas, Baptist pastor, is a brave man. That is why they named this ridge after him—because he is a brave man and because, when he first led his company from the beach, he was up there firing his automatic and pitching hand grenades, and because G Company never has fallen back in all that time.

History-Making Campaign

"They sent us up here," he said, "and I wonder now if they thought we'd ever get here, or stay here if we did, but we knew we would, because we got off that beach

and we beat them at St. Lo and we chased them through
France and Belgium. I guess that's G Company."

When the history of this campaign is written, it will say
that this ridge was the key to Aachen. This is where three
German divisions tried to crack through the shell thrown
out beyond Aachen while the city was being cleaned up.

This has been a horrible place here, and that is why
the captain tells you that sometimes he is scared. When
you came in here a couple of nights ago, in the dark, the
captain was talking on the phone, and when he put down
the phone he said that they had just killed three Germans fifty yards from where you were standing and he
was sitting right then.

"But you know why we've got this candle here," he
had said. "It's because of those guys out there, and I
don't have to tell you what they've got. It's mud. It's deep
in the ground and the water seeps in. It's horrible. It
stinks. It's got lice in it. It's cold, and it's exposed."

Now you were trying to find out from the captain how
men, men who look more like kids, can take that for
forty days and forty nights. You were trying to find out
how they can live like that, in the wet and cold and amid
the dead, when the next moment may be the most horrible they ever have known, and for the most part ask for
nothing more.

The captain was not giving you much of an answer,
but, rather, adding more questions to your own. Then
the door opened and two G.I.'s, dirty and unshaven and
uncertain, came in.

Furloughs for Two

"Sergeant Cuff," the captain said as the G.I.'s stood,
holding their helmets in their hands, in the middle of the
room. "Sergeant Cuff, you and Mullen are going to

Paris. I'm going to send you two to Paris for six days, and how do you like that?"

"Thank you," said Sergeant Cuff, and that was all he said. "Well, you had better like it," the captain said, "and you had better stay out of trouble. Please, for me, stay out of trouble, and, if you get in trouble, find a hole and crawl into it, but have a good time, and bless your hearts."

"Thank you, captain," the sergeant said; Mullen said the same thing, then Sergeant William Cuff of Girardville, Pennsylvania, and Pfc. James Mullen of Pittsburgh, turned around and walked out and Sergeant Cuff's rifle, which was slung over his shoulder, banged on the door as it shut behind them.

First for Leaves

"Two of the best boys I've got," the captain said. "I've said right along that when I got a chance to send somebody back, they'd be the first.

"Wire boys," he said. "They've had to run new lines every day because the old ones got chopped up. One day they laid heavy wire for 200 yards, and by the time Cuff got to the end and worked back, the wire was cut in three places by shell fire.

"Another time, they put a phone up to one of my machine guns, and by the time Cuff got back here to tell me to try the phone, the machine gun had been blown up. So I have been thinking for a long time that they would be the first to have some fun when I could send somebody back."

Out of Hospitals Again

After that you and the captain talked some more about what it is that lets a guy take all this and have enough left to stay another day. The captain hadn't the vaguest idea what it is, and he told you how when these guys are wounded and evacuated to a hospital they sweat out every ambulance that comes in. He said they always are afraid that somebody from G Company might be in it, and when somebody from G Company is in the ambulance they want to know if G Company is still on the ridge and hasn't been driven off.

"Then," the captain said, "somehow they get out of those hospitals and the first thing I know they show up again here, and they're grinning from ear to ear."

The captain said that it probably sounds absolutely crazy that anybody would want to come back to this, but that it is true. He said that probably nobody would believe it, then you talked some more and finally you decided that it was time to get some sleep.

The next morning you were still lying on the sofa cushions that they had placed on the floor, but you had been awake ten minutes when a lieutenant came in. It was dark in the room, so the lieutenant shined his flashlight over on the captain, who was lying in a corner, and when he saw that the captain was awake, too, he went over to him.

"Captain," he said. "Cuff and Mullen say they don't want to go to Paris."

"All right," said the captain. "Get two other guys—if you can."

Capt. Dawson Keeps
Phone Busy

ON DAWSON RIDGE, GERMANY, OCT. 25 (DELAYED).—
When you came in from outdoors, where the Heinie
plane was circling around in the dark and dropping
chandelier flares, and everything of ours up to 90's was
trying to spear it or punch it from the sky, the captain
was still sitting in his wicker chair, and the little radio
was still playing dance music on the table against the
wall.

"Well, if you saw the Krauts go down and they're still
lying there in three weeks," he was saying into the field
telephone, "they're dead. Now you go on and fight the
war, and if you're a good lad I'll let you off with only five
hours in Sing Sing instead of five years, bless your
heart."

Captain Joseph T. Dawson of Waco, Texas, after
whom they named this ridge, sometimes is a very hard
guy, and sometimes he is very soft. He wasn't kidding
about those Krauts, because the lines have been that
close now for many days, our forces having been held up
where they stopped the Germans from driving through

47

to Aachen, and every time our men try to clear the
Heinie dead away they get fired on.

Plans for Attack

"Hello, Colonel?" the captain was saying now into the
other phone. "You promised me you were going to hold
everything down there. All right, bless your heart, I'm
going to hit this damn thing with everything I've got."

There were two field phones on the table—black
phones resting on tan leather cases—and they connected
the captain with his platoons, out in the mud and wet
less than 100 yards away, and with units at his regimental
command post in the rear. Besides the phones and radio
and the maps, on the table were one candle and one
small kerosene lamp.

"I don't give a damn," the captain was saying. "If you
just keep what you got, I'll call you when I get organized."

Then the captain picked up the other phone and
cranked the handle sticking out the side of the leather
case. He started to talk with a lieutenant who leads one
of his platoons, which was at the rear.

"I've decided," he said. "I'm going to take that ground.
Hold on till I get my map."

He Wanted a Piece of Ground

When the captain said that, one of the lieutenants in the
room jumped up from his chair, took the map from the
table and handed it to him. The captain spread it on the
floor between his feet and the lieutenant held a flashlight
on it.

"We are definitely at 653783," the captain said. "I
want to move to 654894. That's right. That's all I want,
just that damn piece of ground. They guarantee they'll

take care of the right flank. Now I want you to stay where you can control it by telephone. O.K.?

"I know that," he said. "If you get small arms fire, you'll overrun it. If you need tanks, we will bring them down and fire point-blank. What time will you be ready to go? I've got a quarter to nine. Right. You be ready to go by 9:30, and if you can't get ready, let me know ahead of time.

Crosby and Judy on the Air

"All right," he said. "You just get me twenty men who'll go down there with me, and I don't want any back-tracking. I want one squad out there in front and twenty men back there ready to go. You get me?"

All the time the captain was talking you could hear our stuff and theirs pounding outside. Every time a big one hit it was like a heavy body being thrown against the door, and you could feel the pressure on your ear drums, and on the radio was some program with Bing Crosby and Judy Garland.

Aside from the radio there wasn't any other sound in the room, because when the captain put down the phone nobody said a word, and you knew that down there at the patrol a lieutenant was picking twenty men. He was picking one man from another, and he knew why, and it wasn't being easy right now for him, any easier than it was for the captain right here.

Bing Has a Few Words

Then the other phone rang—these phones ring very fast and shallow—and the captain picked it up.

"Ed?" he said. "Yeah, it's a little ticklish right now. They're feeling us out and we just killed three or four.

So I'm going to straighten the line. Now push down and take that ground."

When the captain hung up he leaned back in his chair and four lieutenants sat straddling theirs, and for fifteen seconds nobody said a word, and then you were conscious that the music stopped and Bing Crosby was saying something.

"———that wish," he was saying, "is for good luck and speedy travel along the road to victory."

"Shut that off," the captain said.

When he said that one of the lieutenants got up and shut off the radio. Then you were conscious only of noises, most of them sharp, some of them deep, outside. Then the phone rang once more.

Attack Called Off

"Yes, Colonel," the captain said. "But how about 11 o'clock? No, I want to take it out myself. Sure, I can, but if you say—O.K., then, I understand that it's definitely out for tonight."

When the captain hung up, he leaned back in his chair again. He lit a cigarette and the lieutenants just sat there, saying nothing, and then the other phone rang once more and Lieutenant David Houck of Hanover, Pennsylvania, got up and walked over to the table and picked it up.

"That little action is off for tonight," he said. "No, this is Lieutenant Houck. That's right. No attack."

Then the lieutenant placed the phone back on top of the leather case and walked back and sat down again, straddling the chair with his arms on the back and his chin on his arms.

"Thank you, Houck," the captain said.

Following the war's end, Joe Dawson and I exchanged occasional phone calls and correspondence. A geologist in civilian life, he would pursue his calling as a corporate executive and an independent in search of oil fields in Colorado and Texas for more than fifty years. Although diagnosed with prostate cancer in 1991, he returned to Omaha Beach four years later for the Fiftieth Anniversary of D-Day when he was chosen to represent the troops who fought on the Normandy beachheads by introducing the president of the United States, Bill Clinton, at the ceremonies. In 1997 the Joseph T. Dawson Elementary School in Corpus Christi, Texas, was dedicated. On November 28, 1998, he passed away at his Corpus Christi home.

w.c.h., 2002

Little Abie a Hero
on Dawson Ridge

ON DAWSON RIDGE, GERMANY, OCT. 26 (DELAYED).—Pfc. Samuel Freiman is a thin, almost tall guy with an Adam's apple and a pale face and very dark eyes and black hair. He was frightened, and he doesn't remember the incidents of the battle very well, but the other guys in G Company say that he's a terrific fighting man.

"When he raised himself over the top of his hole," Captain Joseph T. Dawson of Waco, Texas, tells you, "Little Abie is shaking so that his helmet is shaking, and his rifle is shaking, and he's shaking all over. His rifle is waving back and forth and up and down, but somehow he brings it down, and he stops it, and he picks them off, one after the other—like that."

That is a kind of G.I. joke they have up here, calling Sammy Freiman of 572 Elton Street, Brooklyn, Little Abie. It is something that means a lot between themselves, and Little Abie is one of them and that is one of the things that make it certain.

The story they like to tell about Little Abie is about the night he killed those Germans. They aren't sure whether it was three or four or five, and Little Abie isn't sure either, because it is so hard for him to remember.

'It Was Just Getting Dark'

But that was ten days ago, the last time the Germans tried to sneak through here to relieve Aachen. Little Abie was in a foxhole with a guy named Mazza, but he doesn't know Mazza's first name or hometown, although they had been living in that foxhole together for more than a month, and when he tells you about it he talks so slowly.

"It was just getting dark and you couldn't see anything," he said. "We heard tanks coming up, and one of the fellows in another hole threw a grenade, but it didn't do any good. Then we saw two Tiger tanks on the other side of a hedge and they were only a few feet away, I think, and they were moving around, and then one went away and the other stopped about twenty-five feet from our hole.

"We didn't know what to do," Sammy said, "and we talked about it in whispers, and we thought about sneaking up and blowing up the track, but the Germans were up and they were talking in English most of the time."

Sammy said he doesn't remember what they were saying.

"Things like that," he said, "they don't bother you. What they were saying you don't remember, but they were talking."

Then the tank pulled away, Sammy said, and it was very quiet for a while. Just now and then you could hear a rifle crack in the dark.

German Looked in Their Hole

"Then a German came and looked in our hole," Sammy said, "and this German said, 'Hello.' We didn't say anything, and he didn't see us, and then he went to another hole and looked in it and said the same thing, and then he and another guy started digging in, just on the other side of the hedge from us."

You interrupted Sammy to ask him how far away the Germans were. He had to think for a while, and then he said they were two feet away.

"They dug for a while," he said, "and then they stopped suddenly, and one of them stuck his head through the hedge because he must have heard us whispering. Then the other guy pulled him back and stuck his own head through, and I let him have it through the head.

"The other guy took off like crazy," Sammy said. "He ran across the road so fast that he hit the barbed wire on the other side and we could hear him scream. Then he started calling the other guy, and then nothing happened for a while."

It must have been quite a while after that, Sammy was saying, when two tanks came back. He said the first tank was about thirty feet away and he was starting to tell you about the second tank when he stopped.

'That's All I Remember'

"What was I talking about?" he said after a while.

"You were saying that the second tank was following the first," you said.

"I guess we'll have to forget that," Sammy said. "I don't remember."

Sammy said he remembered, though, that some Germans got out of the first tank. They were just standing there and not doing anything, he said.

"I shot at them," he said, "but I don't know how many there were, and then the two tanks pulled away and we stayed there all night, and Mazza shot a guy, and the next day we stayed there and that night our guys staged a commando raid and they got us out and that's all I remember."

Dangerous Place, Prospect Park

Sammy Freiman, who is such a thin, pale guy, is 22 years old. He went to Hebrew Tech—that's the Hebrew Technical Institute at 36 Stuyvesant Street, Manhattan—Brooklyn Metal Trades High School, now the Alexander Hamilton Vocational High School, and after he had finished telling you what he could remember, you thought you would talk with him for a while about different things, because you were a new guy for him to talk to.

You found, of course, that it wasn't easy, and so you said something about the weather and you asked him how a guy like him could live in the mud and cold and rain like that for so many days.

"Once, when I was home," he said, and he talked so slowly, "I went to Prospect Park. I was lying down on the grass and I got congestion of the lungs, and I had to go to the hospital. Here I take soaking wet blankets and cover myself and I'm warm and I don't catch cold.

"I can't understand it," he said.

Yanks Slog
Through Rain
to Battle

WITH THE FIRST ARMY IN GERMANY, NOV. 13.—If you
were a painter and could paint only one picture of this
war it would probably be of a battlefield with a dead G.I.
But if you could paint two pictures, that second one
would be of the infantry moving up into the line.

You are thinking now of two of the times you have
seen the infantry moving in. If you tried, you might
write of four or five such instances, but you are thinking
now of two.

The first time was five or six weeks ago. We had already cracked the Siegfried Line once, south of Aachen,
and you had seen that, and now we were going to crack
it again this time through Holland at a place just over
the German border, called Palenberg. We had moved
through Heerlen, and between there and the line there
is a flat plain. This plain must be about a mile long, and
it lies like a table top on a rise in the ground. You cannot
see anything beyond the edge of the plain because the

land all around just ends there, and it is something like what the ancients must have envisaged the world to be.

It was about 7 o'clock in the evening. You remember that because you were hurrying to beat the dark and the dark was winning. There was just about one ounce of daylight left, and it was raining, you thought at the time, as hard as you had ever seen it rain. Along the road across the plain your jeep was soaking and squirting water and mud, and then you caught up with the infantry moving into the line.

Soldiers in Silhouette

The infantry was advancing along the sides of the road, as it always does, in two long, thin lines. All you remember, though, was the line on the right, because it was behind that line that the last light was giving up beyond the plain. If you had been painting that picture, it would have been a picture of blacks and grays. You could not see the men, because it was too dark for that, but you could see their figures, black and glistening a little against the darkening gray, and when the jeep slowed down to go between the columns it was quiet and you could hear the slog of their boots in the mud.

It was farther to the right, then, that our artillery began, but it was so far away that you don't remember ever hearing the sound. It was just like yellow blossoms bursting on a gray wallpaper, sudden but soft, and it was the hour when people hurry home.

It was the hour when everywhere, the world over, people hurry home because they know where they are going whether it's raining or not. You were hurrying because you knew where you were going, but the infantry never knows where it must go.

The second time of which you are thinking now was weeks later and it had been raining for days. You were coming back from the front and you knew where you were going, and you knew where you had been, and you came around a turn in the road. It was the turn in the road that made it so sudden because all at once you were meeting the infantry face to face, and the rain had turned to hail.

The infantry was like it always is, two thin, long lines, one moving along each side of the road. It was two long, thin lines as far as you could see and then it was faces looking into yours.

Your jeep had slowed down again so others could pass it between the lines, and you looked out again to the right, and faces looked into yours. There was one face and then another face, and there were ten feet between them, and they kept on coming. There were rifles slung over shoulders and packs on backs. There were red hands and water and brown eyes and blue, but all the faces looked the same.

You Just Feel Cheap

There were round faces and long faces and rough faces and smooth, and they all looked the same. They all had the same expression because they had no expression at all, because the one looked into yours and was gone and the other took its place and it was that way for a mile.

There were kids with eyeglasses, and it seems now that they hurt the most. There were tough Italian kids who used to work in grocery stores, and there was one kid who, you know, must have come from a white house, part colonial, with a white kitchen with a yellow tile floor and a back yard where he used to kick a football around in the leaves, because his face was that soft.

You have complained to yourself a lot here about having to ride in a jeep day after day when it rains, and when it hails it's worse, and now you wanted to walk. You wanted to walk in the mud and water and in the rain and the hail, and you felt cheap and small, and like a thief, because you didn't know who should have had a right to say that you could ride and they must walk in the rain and the mud and the hail.

They stretched out, these faces, for a mile, you would say now, and when you had passed them the jeep went faster because you knew where you were going, and you knew where you had been. When you had gone many miles it started to snow, and you still saw the faces of the infantry, because the infantry never knows where it must go.

Rabbit
Unnerves Reporters

WITH THE FIRST ARMY IN GERMANY, NOV. 29.—The jeep with the correspondents hurrying to file their stories was boiling back from the front, and the darkness had already won. As the driver started up the winding macadam road, he switched on the little yellow bands that are blackout lights and almost immediately they picked up something small and white, moving up the surface of the road about thirty feet ahead.

It was difficult, under the weak light, to tell what it was, but the driver, Private John Caswell, said it was a rabbit. He comes from Chippewa Falls, Wisconsin.

"Turn on the lights," one of the correspondents said. "Then we can see."

When Caswell turned on the full headlights the figure of the rabbit showed clear in the yellow beam. It was really one of those gray and brown hares, with a white tail that bobbed up and down behind it.

The Rabbit Holds Its Lead

For about a minute everybody in the jeep just kept still and watched the rabbit, which was keeping its distance as the jeep wound up the winding road. Then Private Caswell pulled the jeep toward the middle of the road, and it picked up speed.

With a trailer behind it, lugging recording equipment for one of the radio correspondents, the jeep couldn't go very fast, but as fast as it went the rabbit went just as fast, keeping some thirty feet ahead of it.

It is a long hill, this hill that leads back from the front, and with Caswell trying to pass the rabbit and the rabbit trying to keep ahead of Caswell, one of the correspondents finally suggested that they turn off the lights. Then another said that if they did that they might run over the rabbit, and they finally decided to pull off at the side of the road and then turn out the lights.

Time Out for a Rest

For about thirty seconds the correspondents sat there in the dark, and then Sergeant Russ Jones of the Stars and Stripes suggested that by now they could turn on the lights again and get started. When they turned on the lights, they could still see the rabbit, resting at the side of the road, still about thirty feet ahead, its sides going in and out like bellows, and when the jeep started up the rabbit started up ahead of it in the middle of the road.

The jeep chased the rabbit around one turn in the road and then there was a straight stretch and Caswell put his foot on it. The jeep was going thirty miles an hour now, but the rabbit still kept his distance, his rear legs passing his front ones and his tail flying about a foot off the ground.

"This is beginning to remind me of the dog races in Florida," one of the correspondents said. "They never catch the rabbit there, either."

"This makes me nervous," another one said. "Stop the jeep."

Time Out Again

So Caswell pulled the jeep to the side of the road and stopped it and turned out the lights again, and the correspondents talked the situation over. One of them suggested that they would probably save more time if they just gave the rabbit more time to get away, and so they sat there for about three minutes and then Caswell turned on the lights again, and there was the rabbit, still squatting about thirty feet ahead, his sides still puffing in and out.

"Well, we've gotta get going," one of the correspondents said, so Caswell started up the jeep, and the rabbit wearily pulled himself together and started out ahead again. One of the correspondents said the rabbit looked like he was hitching up his breeches, and now you could see that the rabbit's ears were flat and he was obviously tired.

"All rabbits stay in the light," Caswell said. "It's the same at home."

"Shift into second," one of the correspondents said. "We gotta get past."

The Rabbit Weakens

So Caswell shifted into second and the grinding jeep picked up speed. For a moment the rabbit kept his distance, and then the correspondents could see it weaken in its stride, but it hung on.

"He's game," one of the correspondents said.

"But dumb," another said.

The rabbit was beginning to wobble a little now, from side to side. Now the correspondents could see that the jeep was beginning to gain, and now the rabbit wasn't more than fifteen feet ahead as Caswell pulled the jeep a little to the left to try to get by.

"I don't like this," he said. "He might break in front of the car instead of to the right."

"Keep going," one of the correspondents said, and slowly the gap closed. Finally the right wheel was just about even with the rabbit, but even then he hung on. For several seconds he hung on there without breaking either way, and then he swerved off and pulled himself down into the ditch at the right. At the top of the hill Caswell switched the blackout lights back on and the jeep went on its way.

In the Hürtgen Forest . . .

IN THE HÜRTGEN FOREST, GERMANY, DEC. 5.—The road to the front led straight and muddy brown between the billowing greenery of the broken topless firs, and in the jeeps that were coming back they were bringing the still living.

The still living were sitting in the back seats and some were perched on the back of seats and others were sitting facing forward on the radiators because the jeeps were that crowded. You could see the white of their hasty bandages from far off and there were others of the still living who were on stretchers strung from the front seats to the back and on the radiators too, and the brown blankets came up to their chins.

Along the sides of the road the engineers were walking slowly, passing the flat round platters of their mine detectors just above the mud. Here and there, backed off the road amid the turbulence of the greenery, were the tanks only partly showing and overhead the sky was grey.

When the jeep came to the crossroad the lieutenant—Lieutenant John B. Littlejohn, of Sumter, South Carolina—told the driver to turn left. When the driver turned left the scene was the same except there were no engineers and the tanks were fewer, and the lieutenant said they would find the first one about 400 yards ahead on the right side of the road.

When they had gone about 400 yards the driver pulled the jeep to the right side of the road and stopped. When the jeep stopped the two G.I.s in the back got out, and they went to the trailer and took out the stretcher and picked the first one up.

The first one was right where the lieutenant had said he would be. He was lying face down at the right side of the road with his left arm extended ahead of him, and just below his left shoulder blade was a small round hole around which blood had dried.

The two G.I.s put the stretcher down at the side of the road and rolled this first one away from it, so that he was lying on his back. His eyes were open and there was a small round hole over the left pocket of his field jacket, and the blood had dried around that too. When they rolled him over an unopened K ration carton fell out of the front of his jacket but a hand grenade still clung to it.

"Better take that hand grenade off first," Lieutenant Littlejohn said.

One of the G.I.s—Sergeant Stanley Wahala, of Cleveland, Ohio—took off the hand grenade and put it in his pocket. He then picked up the feet of this first one, and Sergeant Jesse Andrew of French Lick, Indiana, took the shoulders, and they lifted this first one between them and placed him face down on the stretcher, his left arm still stretched out and now suspended in the air.

"He's pretty heavy," Wahala said.

When Sergeant Wahala had backed up to the stretcher and picked up the front end and Sergeant Andrew had picked up the back, they started to walk back to the trailer with this first one between them. When they walked, the head of the dead G.I. lying face down on the stretcher, bobbed up and down with their stride and droplets of thick red blood dripped from his nose with each step and dripped on the stretcher.

When the two G.I.s got to the trailer Corporal Sterling Fuller, of Eatonton, Georgia, the jeep driver, pulled the muddy tarpaulin off and let it drop to the road. The two G.I.s took it easy then, as easy as they could. They lifted the stretcher higher. Very slowly they tipped up the outer edge of the stretcher and slowly eased the dead G.I. off the stretcher and face down onto the bottom of the trailer. Fuller put the tarpaulin back, and the three of them got back into the jeep and drove off.

The second one was also right where the lieutenant had said he would be. He was lying on his back between an old tree stump and one of the tall, fresh green firs from which the top had been blown off. The third one was lying about ten feet away, and each one they took as easy as they could. When the trailer was full they started back.

On the way back the lieutenant and the three G.I.s talked about the Army–Navy football game. They talked about the chicken they were going to have for dinner and about the weather, and when they got back to the collection point the rain had started.

The rain fell soft and grey, and when it fell on the mound of the muddy tarpaulin it ran off in small muddy streams, and Corporal Fuller started to unhook the muddy ropes that held the tarpaulin down.

"You guys better eat first," Lieutenant Littlejohn said. "I don't want you to be late for chow two days in a row."

Of the more than 250,000 words sent by cable or wireless over a period of fourteen months, these were the only ones that did not see print. It was the opinion of the editors that, had this story arrived following the wide coverage of the horror camps, the public would have been better prepared to accept it. I could not quarrel with that then, and I do not now.

w.c.h., 2002

Yank Platoons
Push Off to Attack

WITH THE FIRST ARMY IN GERMANY, DEC. 18.—The Third Platoon of I Company had moved out of the cellar and climbed over the rubble to the place where it would jump off on the attack. The kids of the Second and First Platoons, with their packs on and their rifles beside them, were stretched out together on the straw, awaiting their own turn—apart from the tall, big-faced kid who had shot himself in the hand ten minutes earlier so he wouldn't have to go.

The big kid was lying in a corner, out of the semi-light of the candle, all by himself, holding his arm, with the bandages on the hand, straight out ahead of him. It was the first time you had ever seen a man shoot himself, and he had done a very good job.

While the rest of the men of I Company had been asleep, the kid had taken his rifle and had stood it upright on a little raw-wood table, with the barrel leaning against the wall. Then he had taken a piece of wire from a crate of K rations and wrapped one end around a table leg and hooked the other over the trigger of the rifle.

The kid had done this in the darkness while his buddies were asleep. He couldn't sleep because he was fighting his own battle. You remember now that he was the one who was always talking about the shells landing outside and who had just come back that day from a rest camp where they had sent him for what they had called battle fatigue.

Not So Smart After All

The kid had been talking with the captain. You remembered that he had been talking about batteries for the radio, and had been standing there by the table, leaning against the wall with his right hand over the muzzle of the rifle when he picked up the rifle with his left hand. After the rifle went off the wire was supposed to drop underneath the table.

But the kid hadn't taken into consideration that the wire was stiff, and now it stuck up above the table and everybody knew, although no one said anything directly to him about it, but they all just left him alone.

"Hey, Pill," a G.I. shouted down the stairs, out of the noise of machine guns and shells that was coming in above, "the Third Platoon's moving out now."

Ken Pill of Columbia

He was shouting to Technical Sergeant Ken Pill of Califon, New Jersey, who was baseball captain at Columbia in 1941. Now he leads the Second Platoon.

"Is the first squad here?" Pill asked, and when somebody answered from the darkness in the affirmative he added: "All right, let's go."

The men of the first squad rolled over and got up and went out, one at a time. Another kid got up and went over to a box under a table and took a couple of hand grenades out and started hooking them onto the front of his jacket.

"That's askin' for sudden death," another kid said.

"No, it isn,t," the first kid said.

The G.I. at the top of the stairs shouted down again and the second squad got up and went out. In the back room, a G.I. on the straw said it reminded him of the time between the starter's whistle for you to line up and the moment when the gun goes off.

A Kid Comes Back

"If anybody wants a drink," one kid said, "I've got some hair lotion."

Down the stairs came a G.I. with a rifle in one hand and a couple of radio batteries in the other. He sat down on the straw, near the table with the candle on it where Sergeant George Ricker of Evanston, Illinois, was sitting.

"What are you doing back here?" Ricker asked. "You're supposed to take those batteries out there."

"No," the kid said, "the sergeant said I should come back here."

"What sergeant?" Ricker asked.

"I don't know his name," the kid said. "He said I should come back here."

"Listen," Ricker said, "you know every sergeant in the company. Who was it?"

"I don't know this one," the kid said. "He said I should stay here."

"Look," Ricker said, looking at the kid. "It don't make any difference to me. It's your neck, not mine. You're supposed to take those batteries out there."

"Well," the kid said. "I don't think I can find the company, anyway."

The G.I. at the top of the stairs was hollering something about a line of men coming over the hill. Ricker
shouted for him to take a good look because L Company
was supposed to push off from over there. The first
squad of the First Platoon was getting up now and starting up the stairs.

"They're Krauts," the G.I. at the top of the stairs
shouted down. "There's a long line of them with their
hands over their heads."

"Okay, let 'em come," Ricker said.

The second squad had got up now and started out.
The room was almost empty. Over in the corner the kid
who had shot himself was still lying on his back, holding
the hand with the white bandage on it up in the air. The
runner with the batteries was still sitting on the straw.

"Now I gotta make out the morning report," Sergeant
Ricker said. "I wish this war was over and I was back
home."

DISPATCHES

FROM THE *NEW YORK SUN* (1945)

Questioning Nazi
Captives Is Tough

WITH THE FIRST DIVISION IN BELGIUM, FEB. 2.—Every day now, while it attacks, this division flushes a couple of hundred more German prisoners into its bag, and the word has gotten around here that the interrogation of these Krauts is one of the best shows along the First Army front.

This is so because of the captain who does the interrogation, and it is a shame that you cannot give his name because of censorship reasons. He is what they call a student of human nature, which makes him no slouch as a psychologist, and he is a humorist, too, and you can never tell what is going to happen next because some of these Germans are funny and some of them are tough.

The captain is holding court now in one square room of an abandoned factory building. He sits in a corner with his desk in front of him and there is a window at his left and a white porcelain kitchen range and a couple of chairs around.

When the prisoners come in they stand in front of the desk, and just to see what happens, the captain has a picture of Hitler back of his desk, too. The first prisoner who came in was a paratrooper, a short, stocky little guy with dirty blond hair and a dirty white snow suit.

Would Have Stopped Yanks

The captain asked the prisoner his name and a couple of other questions. Then he held up his hand for the prisoner to stop, and then the captain looked around the room and shook his head.

"He's a hot rock, this guy," the captain said. "He says that if he had been in that position where we threw the weight of that attack, we would never have gotten through. But he says some other club was in there and they gave up too easy."

While the captain talked in English the prisoner stood very still and looked straight ahead. Then the captain started talking with him again in German.

"He's a hot tomato, all right," the captain said, laughing, after he had been talking for about a minute. "He's a Rhinelander and I asked him if he didn't know that all the Rhinelanders have stopped fighting, and he says, 'Yes, I stop fighting now, too.'"

The captain said he'd had enough of this prisoner, and one of the G.I.'s standing there took him out. Almost immediately the door opened and a German lieutenant came striding in.

Lieutenant Salutes

The lieutenant, still wearing his overcoat, strode across the room, stopped in front of the desk, clicked his heels and gave a first class, all-out Nazi salute. What followed was some of the finest and fastest German you ever heard.

"Stop that," the captain said, and he added a few choice expletives, too. "You're finished with that now for all time, so go outside and come in again like a regular soldier."

The prisoner turned around and walked out, opened the door again and walked in. This time he just stood erect before the desk, and kept his hands at his sides.

The lieutenant was in his thirties and wore glasses. He gave his name and then he and the captain talked for quite a while. They talked about the Russian advances, but the prisoner said he hadn't heard how far the Russians had gone, and that got the captain to talking about German atrocities in Russia and Poland, but the prisoner just shrugged his shoulders.

"He's another guy who says he's just a little man," the captain said. "He says any other country should just try to do what his country did. He says there's not another country in the world that could do what Germany has done, and I've just told him that there isn't another country in the world that would want to do what Germany has done."

Wanted to Get to Mons

The captain looked very disgusted. He questioned the prisoner some more and then shook his head.

"Here's another guy who wanted to get to Mons," the captain said. "When the German counter-attack started, they all wanted to get to Mons, because when we liberated Mons the Partisans there killed a lot of Germans, and they all say if they ever get to Mons they will kill every civilian they find there.

"I refuse to try to figure these people out," he continued, and he was very serious. "I used to think I knew these people, but the more of them I talk to, the less I know. Does anybody have any idea what I have to put up with day and night, what I have to listen to day after day?"

With that, the phone on the captain's desk rang. The captain picked it up.

"Oh, hello, Joe," he said. "Have we got prisoners? I'm swamped. Did they give up? Hell, no, we had to fight for them. You what? Okay, Joe. Okay, Joe."

"That was Joe Stalin," the captain said, and he was grinning when he hung up. "He says half the prisoners we get from now on belong to him."

Yanks Plan a Tricky Night Attack

WITH THE FIRST DIVISION IN GERMANY, FEB. 5.—It was while they were squeezing the last of the Germans out of the Belgian bulge, and this division had pulled off thirteen night attacks in a row, and now they said they were going to try the fourteenth and that it probably would be the trickiest of them all.

The trouble was, they said, that the town they were going to try to take lay at the bottom of a hill, and the First Battalion of the Eighteenth Regiment was going to have to attack across 1,500 yards of open ground, down the face of the slope. Besides, the snow was waist-deep, which meant that the infantry would have to ride on top of the tanks, and that would eliminate the element of surprise, because you can hear tanks for a mile.

When you start mixing tanks with infantry you've got a million problems and then two more. It's a little bit like running a church picnic because you've got to think about who is going to ride on what tanks and what you'll do if something happens to these tanks or those, and

---

Part one of a six-part series on the organization of a night attack.

about the timetable and mines, and in the battalion command post the colonel said H hour would be 1 A.M.

The command post was in a very good cellar in the town before the one they were going to try to take. It was warm and there were steel beams and it was 7 o'clock in the evening and the officers in charge of the tanks and the company commanders of the infantry, about a dozen of them, were sitting on the floor while the colonel—Lieutenant Colonel Henry G. Learnard of Arlington, Virginia, was walking up and down.

Start Out Unbuttoned

"It's fifty yards to the left of the road junction," the colonel, a short, wiry little man with wavy hair parted in the middle, was saying. "And be in position by 12 o'clock. We'll have somebody up there to start you off, because there'll be 300 yards between waves.

"That's up there by this tree line," he was saying, pointing with his finger on the map board on the table, leaning against the wall, "and I'll have a guide at that point where you'll deploy. I think it's a very good idea for all successive waves to follow in the tank tracks of the first, in case you hit mines. Also, I would like you to start out unbuttoned, because you are going to have enough of a driving problem as it is."

What the colonel meant was that he thought it would be a good idea for the tankers to keep their turrets open because the visibility wouldn't be very good, especially if they didn't get much moon. That started an argument among the tank guys, and then the colonel said they knew more about it than he did, and it was up to them.

"We'll make up our own minds," the officer who had the medium tanks—Lieutenant Wilburn Sanders of Seguin, Texas, said. "We'll see how it looks when it's time to go."

Every Tank On Its Own

While the colonel was talking, Captain Charles Penick of South Boston, Virginia, had to pump the gasoline lamp every few minutes to keep the white light in the room. The officer in charge of the light tanks—Lieutenant Douglas Banks of Dallas, Texas, said the snow was so deep that he was afraid he'd need the mediums to help push his lights.

"Nix on that," the colonel said. "We'd never get anywhere that way. Every tank has to go on its own, and if it hits a mine or bogs down, the infantry simply has got to unload. Once we get started, we don't stop for anything."

"We've got three tanks that will make it," another officer said. "Those with rubber treads will make it okay, but those with steel treads won't make anything."

What they were talking about was the business of the tanks coming back, once they had dumped the infantry in the town. There weren't enough tanks to carry all of the three companies of doughboys, which meant that after C Company and A Company went in, some tanks would have to come back up the hill to carry B Company, which would be in reserve.

Worried Over Traffic

"It's going to be a helluva traffic problem," the colonel said, and he seemed worried at the time. "I wish we knew more about that damn road."

The colonel was talking about the only road winding down into the town. The road was completely covered with snow, because you can't go sending a bulldozer down into the enemy lines, and then there was the probability that the road was mined, too, so he had decided to turn off the road, just over the brink of the hill, and take to the fields at the left.

"But if we run into things," the colonel was saying, and he was talking about tree stumps and, more important, about mines, "we take to the road and the hell with it. Understand?"

The guys sitting on the floor nodded, and then the colonel sat down on the edge of the table and told Captain Penick to take it from there. The captain stood up and took an aerial photo, with the woods showing black and the snowy fields very white, and he started talking and working over the photo with pencil in hand.

Got Huns an Hour Ago

"You'll assemble here at midnight," he said. "Your columns will join up right here at the point of this wood. Here's your enemy minefield, and don't follow the edge of the wood around too far, because it is mined here, too."

"Is there anything in that house up there?" one of the officers on the floor asked.

"There was a bunch of the Hun in there," the colonel said, because he always speaks of the Germans as the Hun, "but we got them about an hour ago. There'll be Americans in there."

There were other questions, questions about tankers taking bedding along, questions about what streets to cover when they got into the town, questions about food. Then the colonel suggested that everybody had better be getting back to their tanks and companies right away.

The officers stood up and started groping around in corners for helmets and clothes. They stood in groups of two or three, talking with their hands, and then they began to file out.

"Oh, another thing," the colonel said. "This thing is being done in a hurry, without any rehearsal. Remember, there's bound to be some confusion."

Yanks Clear Path
for Night Attack

WITH THE FIRST DIVISION IN GERMANY, FEB. 6.—With the infantry riding on top of the tanks through the deep snow, they were going to attack at 1 A.M. down the 1,500 yards of open slope to try to take the next town.

When you attack at night, the question mark is even bigger than when the thrust is made in the light of day. At the battalion post command, they had had four hours to think of things and sweat it out.

Officers in charge of the tanks and company commanders of the infantry that were to ride with the armored behemoths had left the headquarters at 8 o'clock. At midnight, everybody would start moving out to form up in the woods at the top of the slope. Now, one of the things the colonel—Lieutenant Colonel Henry G. Learnard of Arlington, Virginia—was thinking about was the visibility.

"It's getting lighter all the time, sir," one of the G.I.s said. He had just come into the cellar from outside, and

---

Part two of a six-part series on the organization of a night attack.

he said the moon had not come up yet but it would come up soon and it would be almost full.

Captured Germans

The colonel would sit on the edge of the table and then he would get up and walk over to the barrel-like stove. And then he would walk back to the table again. Just about an hour and a half before they had flushed a half dozen Germans from a house 300 yards down the slope. The colonel said he wanted to know what the prisoners knew about the Germans in the town.

"They don't seem to know anything," Lieutenant Arthur Kiekebush of Winona, Minnesota, said. "They said they had been in the house for two days and they don't know what's going on in town. Their morale is very low."

"Tell them to cheer up," the colonel said. "They'll see the rest of their outfit tomorrow."

"That reminds me," interrupted Captain Charles Penick of South Boston, Virginia. "What about prisoners?"

"The hell with them," the colonel replied. "Once we get started, we are not stopping for anything. We'll pick them up later."

Bulldozer Gets Stuck

The colonel had a bulldozer out to plow over the brink of the hill and down the first 100 yards of the road to where the tanks would turn off into the field. Corporal Jesse Lewis of Raleigh, North Carolina, came in to say the bulldozer was stuck.

"We've got the job done," he said, "but not very good. There are a lot of stumps under the snow in that field."

"The bulldozer is stuck?" asked the colonel. He seemed a little excited at the time. "You've got to get it out of there. Can you get it out?"

"Yes, sir," Lewis assured him.

The colonel asked a couple of questions and Lewis replied "Yes, sir," each time, and then went out.

"This street fighting uses up a lot of ammunition," Captain Penick said. "We can put extra bandoliers on the men."

"Put them on," said the colonel. "They're riding this time."

Two men from a reconnaissance patrol had come in. They were Second Lieutenant Ernest Guldbeck of San Francisco, who wore a white snow suit, and Staff Sergeant John McDaniel of Healdton, Oklahoma, who had no snowsuit. They went over in the corner and sat down with Captain Penick, who had a map before him. You could hear snatches of their conversation.

"There were some Jerries digging in a machine gun right here," the lieutenant reported, designating a point on the map. "It's a miracle we didn't get fired at."

For some reason, that made the colonel think of the correspondent who was going along, and he asked him if he had a weapon. The correspondent explained that he didn't because according to Hoyle or the Geneva Convention or the Marquis of Queensberry or somebody, correspondents in this war are not allowed to carry guns.

"That's up to you," the colonel said, "but I think you're crazy. There'll be plenty of snipers and this street fighting is no church social."

Picked Up Lines

Some of the guys in the cellar had wrapped themselves up in blankets and were lying down on the floor in corners and along the wall. Another kid in a white suit—Corporal Ken Greiner, 61–16 Linden Street, Ridgewood, Long Island—came in and said they had just picked up nine mines that the Germans had strung across the road. He said he had put them in the field to the left of the road.

"Oh, Lord," exclaimed the colonel. "That's right where the tanks turn off the road. You gotta go back there and take them out."

The colonel got on the phone. He talked with the engineers and said he was sending a kid down. He told them to get the mines out of there right away, and then he hung up.

"Those mines are very dangerous," he said to the kid. "They're not supposed to be picked up because they are supposed to be destroyed where they are. But you did a good job. I'm damn glad you found them."

The kid went out. The rumble of tanks moving up the hill to the marshalling point in the woods could be heard.

Men were starting to pull on their sweaters and their jackets over them. One of the officers was going around kicking the shoes of men lying under blankets on the floor.

"C'mon," he was saying, "c'mon! We're moving out now. We're moving out now."

The colonel put on two sweaters and his combat jacket and then his short coat. One of the officers gave him a cup of coffee, which he drank quickly. He put on his helmet, adjusted it and glanced at his watch. It was midnight. He started out.

"Oh, before I go," he paused stopping in the doorway, "will somebody please tell me the name of this town?"

Somebody told him that it was Honsfeld.

Riding into Battle
on a Tank

WITH THE FIRST DIVISION IN GERMANY, FEB. 7.—When the colonel and the major and the captain climbed up from the cellar at midnight the moon was almost full and it was very bright and it seemed as if it was almost in the middle of the sky. It was inevitable, of course, that some one should say it seemed bright enough to be day.

The moon was so bright, in fact, that it washed out the stars and showed the blue in the sky. That is very bright, indeed, and then you had the white snow over everything, and the three officers started walking up the long hill.

It was a mile up the hill, but the road was so steep and the snow so deep that they had decided to walk instead of trying a jeep. They walked single file in the ruts that the tanks had made, and their feet slipped and they began to breathe hard and the road kept winding up between the walls of white on the sagging black of the fir trees on either side.

Up beyond—the road was so steep that it seemed almost overhead—you could hear the grinding, charging

Part three of a six-part series on the organization of a night attack.

noise of tanks maneuvering and the sounds of men. That was where, on the edge of the woods, the men of this First Battalion of the 18th Regiment were crawling from their holes, coming out of the ground, to climb on top of the tanks that would carry them down the 1,500 yards of open slope to attack the next town.

Tanks Carry Infantry

The infantry was going to have to ride on the tanks because the snow was too deep to expect the doughboys to walk that far and have anything left to fight with when they got into the town. The tanks were going to remove all the element of surprise, because you can hear them for a mile, and even now it was a sure thing that the Germans could hear them forming up on the top of the hill.

"Halt," a voice said, in the trees close to the road. "Who's there?"

"Oh-oh," the colonel said. "I forgot to get the password. This is Colonel Learnard."

Captain Charles Penick of South Boston, Virginia, walking behind Lieutenant Colonel Henry G. Learnard of Arlington, Virginia, gave the password in a low voice, and the voice in the trees gave the proper answer. The colonel and the major and the captain started up again and at no time did you see the man whose voice you heard in the trees.

Men Clothed in White

The three officers did not talk but up ahead the sounds became louder and then men began to appear from among the trees alongside the road. They were ghostly, irregular figures, some of them in white, bulging with the equipment on their backs and hanging from their sides, and with rifles slung over their shoulders, and they, too, started to walk up the hill in single files along the sides of the road.

Every once in a while the colonel would stop near men still gathered among the trees and ask them who they were, and they would say "radio" or "liaison" or give the number of their platoon. Then there was a place where the hill leveled off and at the left the trees stopped and there was an open, white field.

Where the field started it was like the top of the world, because you could see nothing but sky beyond, and that was where the tanks started, too. They were mediums and lights, whitewashed so that those farther away were like children's snow forts in the moonlight and the snow, and they were spaced out along the field side and the woods side of the road. Around the tanks stood short ranks of men, loaded with their equipment and waiting, and still the Germans, who must have heard all this down at the bottom of the hill, had not sent in a single shell.

"This is where you get off," the colonel said. "This is Captain Van Wagner here."

Correspondent Gets a Ride

Captain C. C. Van Wagner of Detroit commands A Company and is a tall man. He said he'd give this correspondent a guide to lead him to the tank on which he was going to ride.

"Don't worry," the colonel said, "but don't forget to duck. Once these kids get going, nothing will stop them, because they're fighting for places to keep warm. They've been living in holes, but there are cellars in that town."

That was all the colonel said, and he and his two officers started walking on. They were going up to a dugout

on the edge of the woods, to run the initial stage of the
attack from there, and then they were coming in with B
Company, which was in reserve.

The guide was Pfc. Paul Lamprecht of Roselle Park,
New Jersey. He takes long steps and he walks very fast,
and he went on up the road and where the woods come
to a point, right on the edge of the hill, he turned
sharply to the right, and there were more tanks lining
both sides of the road that runs back from there.

All along the road now was the deep noise of the tank
exhausts. It was soft and deep in the white night, like the
voice of good motorboats idling, rolling slowly at a wharf,
and still the Germans had not thrown in a single shell.

Ring Around the Moon

Overhead there was a big, faint, white ring around the
moon now, and between the tanks were the dark figures
of the helmeted kids, helping one another into packs and
straining to get machine gun tripods up on their shoulders. The dark shoulders and heads of tankmen were
protruding from the turrets of the tanks, and behind the
turrets, standing in clusters on the sloping white tops of
the tanks were six or eight or nine darker figures, the infantry waiting.

Lamprecht went past the medium tanks to the lights,
and then he stopped at one and said that this was it, and
turned around and started back the way he had come.
The kids on top of the tank looked down and one of
them said hello.

Talked About Russian War

There were four tank guys in leather helmets walking
around the tank to keep warm. One of them was the as-

sistant driver, Private Alfred Schmieder of 115 Bushwick Avenue, Brooklyn, and he was eating a K ration, and another was the driver, Sergeant Russell Diehl of Mount Morris, Illinois, and he kept running up and down the road about sixty feet each way to keep warm.

"Let me go in, Coach," he'd say every time he'd get back to where the others were standing. "Please, Coach, put me in the game."

There was a long wait, and the guys talked about the Russian war. It got to be 1 A.M., which was supposed to be H hour, and nothing happened, and then it got to be 1:10, and one of the kids said something must have happened, and then a G.I. came running down the road.

"Load up quick, load up quick," he hollered. "We're kicking off."

The tank guys started to crawl up onto the tank and down through the turret, and in back the infantry guys started to squat down and make room for one more. Up ahead you could hear the sound of the tanks moving now, moving toward the brink of the hill, and then the tank, about sixty feet ahead, started to move, and it was as undramatic as that, because still the Germans hadn't thrown in a single shell.

Kids Cling to Tanks on
Way to Battle

WITH THE FIRST DIVISION IN GERMANY, FEB. 8.—It was
1:15 A.M. when, under the full moon and through the
waist-deep snow, the white tanks with the infantry clinging to their tops pushed across the flat shoulder of the
hill and nosed down and started across the 1,500 yards of
open slope to try to capture another town.

There were two waves but they went in a single line.
There were about a dozen tanks and then 300 yards and
about a dozen more, and then there was still another infantry company of this First Battalion of the Eighteenth
Regiment waiting at the top of the hill in reserve.

This, you might think in reading about it back home,
was what this war is all about. If you have a map in your
newspaper, this was the very point of the arrow showing
the direction of the American advance. If you have in
mind a great pyramid of sweat and coal and steel and
loneliness and gasoline and no meat and another War
Bond tomorrow, this was the tip, the point of that, too,
and yet all it was, really, was one tank following another

Part four of a six-part series on the organization of a night attack.

with a bunch of kids, cold and a little taut, clinging to their tops.

That is all that it is, really, on the top of a tank, because that is where all reason stops. Back in the battalion command post the colonel and the major and the captain and the rest will worry a lot. They will worry about how many Germans there may be in the town and what kind of guns they've got and whether they're good troops or not. They will worry about minefields and artillery and whether the Germans this time will stay and fight. But it isn't like that on top of a tank.

'Here We go,' Says Kid

On the top of a tank in the second wave it doesn't matter much whether the first wave will catch the small arms fire and the second wave the artillery when the Germans wake up. It was this same kind of thing yesterday and it probably will be the same kind of thing tomorrow, and once the tank starts to move it doesn't matter at all.

"Here we go," one of the kids said, flatly, meaning nothing at all, and that was the only thing anybody said for five minutes or more.

When the tanks started they made a lot of noise. The ones up ahead spit and ground and shot out blue flames. Then when the light tank started there was only its own noise and nothing more.

The tank lurched back and started ahead, and there wasn't much room. On the back of the light tank there is about the space of two bridge table tops, and that isn't much for six guys when one of them has a radio on his back, and they've got carbines and gas masks and canteens and overcoats and extra bandoliers.

By the time the light tanks got to the brink of the hill the mediums were firing down below. They were down there in a gray-blue haze that hid the tanks and the town, and there was a little island of pines sagging with snow in between, and from beyond that island there came no sound over the sound of the tank with the six guys.

Tracer Bullets Fired

There were red tracer bullets from the tanks, some spitting, some arching lazily across the sky. Cutting across them were white tracers from the Germans, and halfway down the hill on the left was a wooden barn that burned bright orange from top to bottom and smoked orange and reflected orange across the deep snow.

All the light tank did was follow the one about sixty feet ahead. It followed it from the road into the field to the left, rocking, lurching and making the guys on top grab one another and grab the tank and hang on.

"I'm frozen," one of the kids said. He was Pfc. Eugene B. Knueve of Milan, Michigan, and he was sitting facing forward, with other guys sitting on him facing back, and he said he didn't think he could move his leg.

The tank stopped. Nobody asked why. It started up again and then there was a very sharp, quick whistle and the six guys seemed to tighten as one, and then there was a sharp crack like somebody banging two table boards together just once, and the guy on the left made a move.

Lieutenant Makes a Move

The guy on the left was a second lieutenant, and he was the only one who had on a white snowsuit. All he did was to make a move, it seemed, toward the side of the tank, when the guy next to him grabbed him by the arm.

"No you don't, bud," he said, and his voice was very steady and very low. "Stay here."

"I'll get squashed," the lieutenant said, and his voice was very high. "They'll mash me right here."

"Stay here," the other guy said, and his voice was still very steady and very low. "Otherwise you'll get killed."

The other guy was just the first sergeant, but he landed in North Africa a long time ago. He was First Sergeant Thomas J. Milan of Bayonne, New Jersey, and the tank lurched and rocked on.

"Over there," one of the other kids said, and he pointed to the left and about forty yards away. Where he pointed was a black hole in the snow where a German shell had landed, and around it the snow was blown and black and the tank lurched and rocked on.

The lieutenant in the white snowsuit had squirmed around so he was facing the other guys and he raised his head and looked over at the other side of the tank. He asked if there was any room over there.

"There's no room over here," one of the kids on the other side said. "You'd better stay where you are, sir."

G.I.s Look for Town

"Can you see the town yet?" Milan asked, because he was facing the other way. The radioman—Pfc. Earl Weir of McPherson, Kansas—said he could not see the town, just tracers and what looked like a fire or two.

"We oughta be near the town," Milan said. "It can't be much further now."

The tank rocked on. It made its own noise, and that was the only noise you could hear, and all it did was to follow the tank ahead.

"Can you see the town?" Milan asked again. "We oughta be getting near the town."

"I can see buildings," the lieutenant in the white suit said. "God, I hope it's the town."

About 100 yards ahead, by about the fourth tank, there were buildings, gray in the moonlight, on both sides. They seemed to be half-buildings, without roofs, and behind them was an orange glow, and you could see a few tracers here and there and then the guy standing in the turret of the tank—Staff Sergeant William Rensi of Piney Fork, Ohio—who was the tank commander, turned around.

"Get ready to unload," he said, and then he turned back and the guys on the back stirred a little but did not move.

The tank rocked on. There were buildings now, with white snow between them and on them, on both sides, and then the tank stopped with a jerk, and ahead there were sounds of many men's voices.

"Unload, unload!" somebody shouted, and one of the guys on the back of the tank said "Unload," and, going over both sides and down the back with their carbines in their hands, they tumbled off into the snow.

Lack of Proper
Winter Equipment
Costs U.S. Lives
in Attack on Town

WITH THE FIRST DIVISION IN GERMANY, FEB. 9.—There were about a hundred houses in the town that the First Battalion of the Eighteenth Regiment was entering in the culmination of a night attack across 1,500 yards of open ground through snow so deep that the infantry had to ride on top of the tanks.

Perhaps it might be nice to say that there were a few more houses, out of respect for the guys who at 5 minutes to 2 in the morning jumped and slid and fell off the tanks in the moonlight and started out, black figures in the snowy streets between the black houses, to clean out the town.

That is something America has got to live down. She has got to live down the fact that this winter she has sent her kids out black against the white snow and that be-

Part five of a six-part series on the organization of a night attack.

cause of this some of them have been wounded and some of them have been killed, because she didn't think she was going to have to fight a winter war.

When everybody was shouting "Unload," and the kids tumbled off the tanks, some of them fell on their faces in the snow and some of them sat right down. The snow was very deep and loose because it was very cold, and when the kids scrambled along on their hands and knees it shifted under them as they tried to get to their feet and then they were on their feet, starting out in two long lines.

White Tanks Roll Up

One line went up each side of the street, and here and there one of the white tanks went up between the black lines. Before they started, each company and each platoon and each squad knew where they were going and what houses they were going to take, because they had studied aerial photos of the town, and yet it always looks so different when you get into a town.

When you get into a town you find that many of the houses don't have roofs and most of them don't have windows and doors, and they look very ominous and dark while you are very black yourself, moving along in the moonlight against the white snow. All the time, up ahead and on the sides, you can hear that chat-chat and crack of small arms, and there is always the possibility that at any moment it may start from the windows of any one of these houses and just work right up and down along the lines of guys strung out along the street.

So this reporter ran along behind the guy ahead, bent over double, stopping, running between the open spaces, and falling flat in the snow when the zing-zing of the rifle bullets sounded somewhere in the air. Every once in a while a couple of guys will break off the line and make a run for a house, and that's the way it was in this town, too.

Warns Young Soldier

"Don't," one of the guys in the line hollered, and then he swore and hollered louder. "They'll cut you down."

One of the kids in a snowsuit—one of perhaps a half-dozen who had snow suits—was running toward a front door. It was just a blacker hole in the front of the black house, and he was silhouetted in the door for a moment and then was inside, and the kid in the line who had hollered called him a very strong name.

Up at the end of the street a barn was on fire. The whole sky seemed to be lighted orange over the barn, which was a pulsating orange thing itself. That made the snow in the street orange, too, and with the rest of the sky so blue in the moonlight it looked like one of those overdeveloped color movie films.

The line kept going forward, running, stopping and then just before it got to a corner where there was a church set back at the left, there was the brrrp-brrrp-brrrp of a German burp gun. The German gun is an automatic weapon that is named after the way it sounds, and the line stopped, the guys resting, many of them on their knees, breathing hard and their breath hanging in the air.

Call for Machine Gunners

"Machine gunners," somebody up ahead said, and the words came stronger and then weaker as they passed down the line. "Machine gunners, machine gunners. Machine gunners wanted up ahead."

The machine gunners came up. There were a couple of kids carrying the guns and a couple of kids with the tripods on their backs, and they ran between the lines of waiting, kneeling men. They slipped and stumbled when they ran in the deep snow and then there was a wait and then you could hear the slow chut-chut-chut-chut of the American machine guns, which always sound like heavy-headed woodpeckers working out on a hollow log, and then you didn't hear the burp gun any more.

The line started to move again and a lieutenant or whoever came running up the middle of the street. He was hollering as he ran along.

"For God's sake, keep spread," he was hollering. "Keep your interval. Keep spread."

Soldiers Spread Out

The lieutenant, or whoever he was, ran up for some distance and then ran back. The kids in the line let those ahead of them get farther away, until there was about twelve or fifteen feet between each, and there was always the sound of small arms fire, and then somebody would say "sniper," and the word "sniper" would travel up and down the line.

All this time, kids were dropping off and making runs for houses on both sides. Then down the road between the two lines of Americans the Germans started to come.

The Germans had their hands over their heads. The first one had on a white helmet and the second was bare-headed but had on a white snow suit, and there must have been a dozen of them in the line. Behind them, slipping, trudging after them, was an American kid with a tommy gun and on both sides of them the two lines of Americans, stopping, starting, running, went on.

At a corner there was a lot of confusion. That was where C Company went off to the right, and A Company was to take that part of the town to the left. Even in the moonlight, the kids couldn't recognize each other very well and there were a lot of cries for platoons and shouts of "Who's this?" There was some cursing and a few arguments, and over this the sound of some small arms fire, and then the two companies split up and started off, one of them in one direction and the other in the other.

They worked up both sides of the streets, some of them dropping out to look over a house here, others to look over a house there. Most of them just got tired from running bent over in the deep snow, and most of them never did get a chance to fire their guns because the only Germans they saw were the ones coming out with their hands up.

But there were Americans killed here and some Americans were wounded, although the Germans really didn't put up a tough fight. Now it is somewhat of a shame that there aren't more names to go with this story, but at a time like that there is no way of taking notes, and besides, if you were to ask a kid his name under such circumstances he might think you were crazy.

In fact, there was one lieutenant who was standing with a group of G.I.'s in the shadow of a building. You asked him if that building was going to be the company command post and he asked who you were and you said: "Newspaper man."

"Oh, Lord," he said, and then he turned his back and walked away.

Yanks Work Over a German Town

WITH THE FIRST DIVISION IN GERMANY, FEB. 10.—Before the attack started, the colonel had said that the kids would fight well because what they would be fighting for would be the houses in the town. They had been living in holes dug down through the snow and blown out of the ground, and so when they went through the town at 2 o'clock in the morning, rooting out the Germans, killing those who fought back and capturing those who didn't, what they were really fighting for first of all were the houses in the town.

The two company commanders had orders from the colonel to find a good cellar for the battalion command post, and then they had to find cellars for their own command posts, too. Meanwhile they would go on cleaning up the town and then the town would be outposted and then the kids would find cellars of their own.

"Has this house been searched?" the captain asked. It was five minutes to three and, standing out in front in

---

Part six of a six-part series on the organization of a night attack.

the moonlight on the snowy street the kids said it had not been searched very well.

The captain gave orders for the house, which hadn't any windows, to be searched upstairs. Then he took his flashlight and went down into the cellar with his first sergeant—First Sergeant Thomas J. Milan of Bayonne, New Jersey—and looked around and said that would be his command post there.

The cellar was so low and long, with an arched ceiling, that it looked like a cave. There was a small stove there but it had gone out, and it was very cold, and there were a half-dozen straw mattresses on the floor, on which the Germans had been sleeping, and Milan groped through his musette bag and found half a candle and lighted it and stuck it on the seat of a chair.

Reached Objective

Meanwhile the troops outside were cleaning up the town. You could hear the steady chut-chut of our machine guns and occasionally a short blast from a German burp gun, the rumble of a tank, and now and then the crack of a single rifle.

"So this guy lets go from this window," one of the kids was saying. They were coming down into the cellar now and talking about the fire they had drawn and the fighting they had seen.

"Get that radio going and tell them we've reached our objective," the captain—Captain C. C. Van Wagner of Detroit—said. Pfc. Robert Malark of Cranston, Rhode Island, had set the radio up on a chair and was monkeying around it with a flashlight and a pocket knife.

There was a nice fight going on upstairs between a German in a building somewhere and some Yanks, and then a tank rumbled up. A lieutenant came in and took off his helmet and started to talk.

Watching Burp Gun

"There is this burp gun going away," he said, "with the two guys watching it and I ask them what they're doing. 'Oh, we're watching this burp gun,' one of them says, 'we're going to knock it out after a while.' Can you imagine that?"

"Boy," one of the others said, "I sure wouldn't have wanted to have been a Heinie sitting in this town."

It was very cold in the cellar, almost as cold, it seemed, as outside. When the kids talked you could see their breath, and a lieutenant came in and reported to the captain and said he and another platoon commander were having an argument as to who was in whose territory.

The captain got out his aerial photo of the town, and when he opened it with the lieutenant, the lieutenant said he had men here and there, and here was the railroad track, and the captain said he was right.

"Besides," he said, "any house you grab in this town is yours."

Shelling Begins

The lieutenant went out and a major came in. The major told the captain he was in the wrong house, and when the captain looked bewildered the major told him that C Company had its command post right across the street and you couldn't have two command posts on the same street.

So everybody in the cellar picked up everything and Milan snuffed out the half-candle and put it in his pocket and started out. Right then the first German shell came in, which is something else that happens with these towns.

First the Americans will shell a town, stopping just before the attack starts. Then there will be no shells while the fight is going on in the town and then, when they realize that they're kicked out, the Germans start shelling the town and they keep shelling it for hours or days or however long it takes to push them out of range, which is why there isn't much left of these towns.

The captain went up the street, looking for another house, and there was a G.I. marching about a dozen German prisoners down the road in single file. Shells were whining and crumping in regularly now, but the German prisoners never ducked, and they just kept marching along in good rhythm, with their hands overhead, slipping a little in the deep snow.

There were a couple of houses burning which, with the moonlight, lighted things up pretty well, and as the G.I. marched the prisoners along other G.I.s kept coming out of houses herding three or four more Germans ahead of them and motioning them to get into the marching column. By the time the G.I. got to the battalion command post there must have been more than thirty Germans in the line.

Massages His Foot

In the battalion command post, Lieutenant Colonel Henry G. Learnard of Arlington, Virginia, was standing with his back to a kitchen range. There were officers and G.I.s sitting around on chairs and on the floor, and one lieutenant had one shoe and stocking off, and was massaging his foot with his hands.

"My feet have been frozen for two weeks now," he said, and he wasn't kidding.

The colonel looked very tired and pale but was very happy. He said everything had gone well and he guesses they'd get more than 100 prisoners this time.

It was 4:30 A.M., and the colonel said that only one thing was worrying him. He said he had a lieutenant out looking for a good house for the regimental command post, which would be moving down later in the day. He said he'd had orders from the regimental commanding officer to get a good house, so you see that what they had really been fighting for first of all were the houses in the town.

Old German Gets
in Colonel's Hair

WITH THE FIRST ARMY IN GERMANY, FEB. 13.—There were still some American squads working through the town flushing the last Germans from the cellars here and there, and in the battalion command post the colonel was worrying whether the Germans had managed to blow up the bridge or not.

The command post was in one of the few houses in town that were untouched. It had been set up in the kitchen where there was a big flat coal stove and two tables and some benches against the wall, and guys came stumbling into the room to make reports and to sit down and to fall asleep on the benches and on the floor because they had been at it for twenty-four hours.

The colonel was sitting on a bench with his legs stretched out straight in front of him and listening to the field radio. On the radios, the platoons were yapping back and forth about what progress they were making and what they were finding, and sitting very quietly on the bench between a couple of G.I.'s was a civilian smoking a pipe.

He's a Hun to the Colonel

The civilian was the guy that owned the house. He had a gray cap on his head, and he was about 65 years old with a round face and a handlebar moustache. Every time somebody would come in, he would nod at the G.I. and smile at him and follow him around the room with his eyes and his pipe. Every once in a while, a G.I. would smile back and try to talk with the old man.

"Parlez vous francais?" the G.I. would say.

"Nein, nein," the old man would say. "Versthen sie nicht deutsch?"

The G.I. would usually look very dumb and shrug his shoulders and look around the room. Invariably the colonel would look up about then and say not to pay any attention to the old man.

"He tells me he likes Americans," Lieutenant Arthur Kiekebush of Winona, Mississippi, said once. "He says he hates German soldiers and is glad we've come."

"He's a Hun," the colonel said. "He's the same as all the Huns.

Shells Don't Sound Kaput

The man was sitting there watching the colonel and the lieutenant talking back and forth. Whenever somebody looked at him he would nod his head.

"All German soldiers are kaput," the old man said in German, and he kept nodding and smiling around the room. Lieutenant Kiekebush translated that but unfortunately one of the shells the Germans were sending in landed just then somewhere in the rubble outside.

"Sure the Germans are kaput," the colonel said. "It's autumn, and those leaves are falling out there."

The colonel went back to his radio. He reported that an outfit on the battalion's right was catching it in the neck of the woods. He said he could hear the battalion commander screaming that he had just lost one of his officers in one company and was trying to reorganize.

Missing—A Pair of Shoes

"And it must be those self-propelled guns that got away from us here," the colonel said. "They moved up that road, and they are probably firing into that woods now."

The colonel went back to his radio. The door opened and another old man came in. He was about 80 years old also with a mustache, and he bent over almost double. He had on a brown corduroy jacket and riding breeches and a pair of rubber boots.

The old man who had just come in started looking around the room and then he went over near the colonel and got down on his hands and knees and started crawling under the bench. He had been crawling around the colonel's legs for more than a minute before the colonel even noticed him, as he was so busy listening to the radio.

"Who's this guy?" the colonel said, taking the radiophone away from his face with a jerk and pulling his legs up under him. "Now what's this guy doing?"

"He's looking for his shoes," Lieutenant Kiekebush said. "He can't find his shoes."

The Colonel Is Exasperated

"Look, Kiekebush," the colonel said, "we've got these rooms downstairs, and they've gotta stay out of here. They can stay in the cellar or upstairs."

The old man had found his shoes, and Lieutenant Kiekebush went out. The old man stood in a corner holding his shoes in his hand and looking around the room, and there was a young lieutenant from the engineers who was standing in front of the old man on the bench and talking with him.

"Verstehen sie mines?" the lieutenant was saying in mixed German. The old man was looking back up at him and smiling and nodding his head, and the colonel looked up and wanted to know what was going on now.

"He says he knows where the Germans planted mines around here," the lieutenant— Lieutenant Donald Allen of Malden, Massachusetts—said. "I want to get him to show me on the map where the Germans planted their mines."

"Well, of all the ———," the colonel said, "I never heard anything as silly as this. What does that old geezer know about mines?"

More Distractions

"You can never tell what he might know," Lieutenant Allen said, and he went back to talking with the old man. Then he got out his map case, and the old man stood up.

First the old man took a handkerchief from his back pocket and cleaned his glasses. Then, he refilled his pipe and lighted it. Then he took the map case up in his hands and started turning it around. First he turned it one way and then he turned it another.

"He can't read the map," one of the kids said. "Try him on an aerial photo."

The kid was Sergeant Christopher Cornazzani of 298 Quincy Street, Brooklyn. He unrolled an aerial map of the town and held it up in front of the man.

"That's stupid," the lieutenant said. "How can an old man like this read an aerial photo?"

"This whole thing is stupid," the colonel said. "What does this old geezer ———."

Lieutenant Kiekebush came in and the colonel looked up. The room was so crowded now that Kiekebush had to step over the G.I.'s.

"I explained to the two women and the boy," he said. "They want to know if they can come in now and help the old man put on his shoes."

"THE MORNING THEY SHOT THE SPIES" AND OTHER FEATURES

(After the War)

The Morning
They Shot the Spies

from *True*, 1949

We skirted Liége and turned east on the road that leads past the Belgian forts dug into the ground. It was cold. It was two days to Christmas. It was still early and the mist hung over the fields and, in some places, over the road. I remembered when we went through here with the tanks in September. The sun shone every day and it was warm then, and the Germans were running for the Rhine. It was hard to find Germans then, and when the Americans found them the Germans quit easy and it seemed that the war would be over by Christmas and maybe we would be home.

"Stay on here," I said to the driver. "After we go through Herve I'll tell you. I remember it's on the left-hand side of the road."

When we went through Herve the people were just starting the day. There were a few of them on the street—a woman in a shawl pouring a pail of steaming, cloudy water into the cobblestone gutter, and a couple of workers walking along the sidewalk, their breaths showing, the collars of their old jackets turned up and their hands in their pants pockets. They paid no attention to us.

"That's the place up on the left," I said to the driver. "I can remember it."

I could remember the wall along the road, and the opening in it. I could remember the low stucco barracks on the other three sides of the dirt quadrangle, and we drove past the guard at the gate and across the frozen yard. The driver put the jeep in with some others at the far end, and we got out, stiff from the cold, and walked back across the dry, hard dirt to what looked like the office.

There were some M.P. personnel working in there at desks behind a guard rail. There was a potbellied stove at the back, and we walked over to it, standing around it and taking the heat and talking about it until a young lieutenant came over and asked us if he could help us.

"We're here for this spy thing," I said.

"Oh," he said. "Then you go across there to the mess hall."

He pointed and you could see through the glass in the far door the building that he meant.

"What time is it coming off?"

"I'm afraid I don't know," the lieutenant said. "This place is in a mess. Just go over there. I'm sure that someone will tell you in plenty of time for you to see it."

We went out and walked across the quadrangle toward the building. The side showing on the quadrangle was made up almost entirely of wide sliding doors. One of them was open and, looking in, I could see some people who had driven down from the Ninth Army at Maastricht.

I judged this place had been a stable when the Germans had used it. Now the Americans were using it as a mess hall, and a couple of the people from Ninth Army

were sitting on the benches, their backs to the long tables, while the others moved around, stamping their
feet, their hands in their pockets. There was no heat in
the place.

The Ninth Army people didn't know anything. I could
tell from the way they talked that they didn't know the
censors had put a stop on this, that you couldn't write
about it, but I wasn't going to tell them.

In a few minutes a captain came in. He was quite
young and freshly shaven, and he looked cleaner than
anything else around the place. He was smiling and he
went around introducing himself and shaking hands. He
seemed to be trying to be the perfect host, and his en-
thusiasm and his friendliness made me a little annoyed
with him.

"I suppose," he said, "that you gentlemen understand
about the censorship of all pictures."

"We know all about it," one of the photographers said.
"You don't have to worry about it."

"And I suppose you also understand," the captain said,
"that nothing is to be written about this."

I felt a little sorry for the writers who had come down
from Maastricht. It came to them as a surprise. They
started to put up a real kick, but they must have known it
was a waste of time to argue.

"But I thought they wanted a lot of publicity about it,"
one of them said. "I thought they wanted it to get back
to the Germans so they'd stop this sneaking guys into
our lines."

"I don't know anything about that," the captain said.

"Then why didn't they tell us?" somebody else said.
"Why didn't they tell us before we wasted our time driving way down here in this cold?"

"I'm sorry," the captain said. "You know as much
about it as I do."

Several of them said they would leave, talking about it among themselves, but they all stayed. To put an end to the argument someone asked the captain what he knew about the prisoners.

"All I know," he said, and you could see him thinking about what he had rehearsed, "is that they were picked up at night inside our lines in an American jeep. They were wearing American uniforms, and had a radio. They hadn't accomplished anything, as they had just entered our lines when they were picked up.

"One of them is an out-and-out Nazi. He's the short one. The other two, I believe, are innocent of any original intent of spying. One of them is a farm boy from Westphalia. He's quite simple and, I think, quite honest.

"The story he tells—and I'm inclined to believe it—is that several weeks ago, before this German counteroffensive started, a call went out for men who speak English. He volunteered, he said, because he thought it would be a soft job back at headquarters on propaganda or prisoner interrogation or something like that. The next thing he knew, he was in an American uniform and in an American jeep and heading for our lines. He said there was nothing he could do, and I don't suppose there was, because they always put one Nazi in with the weak ones to see that they keep in line."

We stood around the captain listening, and some of the Ninth Army people were taking notes. I thought the captain was very efficient. He was telling us all that he could.

"We've never done anything like this before," he said. "It's rather a messy thing, and we'll be glad to get it over."

"Then what are we waiting for? We were notified this thing would be at nine-thirty."

"I don't know," the captain said. "I imagine they may be waiting to see if there's any other word from SHAEF.

I suppose they want to be sure SHAEF hasn't had a change of mind about it."

"Then how long do we have to wait?"

"I haven't found out," the captain said, "but it should be within a half hour."

"How about the prisoners? Can you tell us how they're taking it?"

"All right," the captain said. "The chaplain has been seeing two of them, but the Nazi wants nothing to do with him. We have some Wehrmacht nurses in the next cell, and last night the three asked that the nurses be allowed to sing some Christmas carols for them."

"Then they know they're going to be shot this morning?"

"Yes. The chaplain informed them last night."

"Was the request for the carols granted?"

"Of course."

"What carols did the nurses sing?"

"I don't remember exactly," the captain said, "because the only one I recognized was 'Silent Night.' We had to stop them after a while."

"Why?"

"Because they were disturbing our troops."

I wondered if the captain knew that "Silent Night" is an Austrian carol that the rest of us borrowed.

"We can go now," he said. "Keep together and follow me. When you get there, keep about twenty-five or thirty feet back. There will be an M.P. stationed there, and you are to keep behind that line. That goes for the photographers, too. Also, once you get there you will have to stay because no one will be allowed to leave."

"In other words," one of the Ninth Army people said, "if we want to back out, we have to back out now."

"That's right," the captain said, smiling.

I thought about backing out and I wished no one had mentioned it. I was starting to feel a fear, and we followed the captain out and across the quadrangle. We walked in a straggling group past the place where the jeeps were parked, and we took a path that ran along, on the left, the side wall of a low, gray stucco building. On the right there was a field, gray with frost, and the path was rough with frozen footprints. I wondered if the prisoners knew now how close they were to it.

The path we took led down into a field behind the stucco building. The field sloped a little away from the building, running down to a barbed-wire fence. Beyond that the ground dropped rather suddenly, and you could see into a valley, filled now with the mist. We walked maybe fifty feet into the field, the captain taking us around several M.P.s standing at ease in the field, and then we turned and faced the back wall of the building.

The wall was about eight feet high. About three feet out from it and spaced about fifteen feet apart were three squared posts stained brown. The postholes were new.

We stood there in a group, an M.P. to our left, looking at the posts. I looked at the ground, frost-white, the grass tufts frozen, the soil hard and uneven. I wondered if it is better to die on a warm, bright day among friends, or on a day when even the weather is your enemy. I turned around and looked down into the valley. The mist still hung in the valley, but it was starting to take on a brassy tint from the sun beginning to work through it. I could make out three white farm buildings on the valley floor—a little yellowed now from the weak sunlight—and I could envision this, in the spring, a pleasant valley.

This view I see now, I said to myself, will be the last thing their eyes will ever see. I looked at it intently for that reason. I thought of the human eye and of its complexity and its marvelous efficiency. I found myself thinking only of the farm boy, the Westphalian, for whom this would be the last room, the last view, and I turned back to the others.

That was when we heard the sound of marching feet. I turned and I saw them coming around the corner of the building, along the path we had taken.

There was, first, an M.P. officer. Behind him came the first prisoner and I knew at once that he was the one the captain had described as the farm boy from Westphalia. Behind him, in twos, marched eight M.P.s, then another prisoner, eight M.P.s, the third prisoner, and eight more M.P.s. The boots of the M.P.s shone with polish and on their helmets the lettering and bands were a fresh, new white. The prisoners wore American combat jackets over fatigue jumpers like those that garage mechanics sometimes wear—more green than khaki—and there was a stripe of light blue paint down the front of each leg.

So that technically they won't be shot in American uniforms, I thought. They had to give them something to wear.

It was difficult to march well over the rough, frozen ground. You could tell this by the way the tips of the rifles wavered in the lines. I watched them, thinking of the wonders of the walking process, of the countless steps we give away so cheaply for needless reasons until there are no more. Now the column seemed to be marching so quickly.

They had turned off the path and now moved across in front of us, between us and the wall. When they reached a point where the Westphalian was opposite the last post, the officer at the head shouted and the column stopped, the men marking time, the feet of the prisoners a part of the rhythm. Then he shouted again and the feet stopped and the column stood at attention. Both times that he shouted I noticed the Westphalian looked down and back nervously at the feet of the M.P.s behind him as he obeyed the orders.

He is a good soldier, I thought. At a time like this he is worrying about being in step, and he is afraid that he is not catching the commands. You have to give him something for that, I thought, and I looked at him carefully. He was the one all right—tall, big-boned, long-faced, with long arms, his fingers red and just showing below the sleeves of the American jacket that fitted him poorly and made him seem all the more pathetic.

There was no doubt about the second one either. He was the one the captain had described as the Nazi. He was short, about five feet four, and he had a high, bulging forehead and flat, black hair and he wore black-rimmed glasses. He stood very erect, his face set as stiffly as his body.

The third one did not impress me. He was well built— by far the best looking of the three—and he had black, curly hair. In my mind he was something between the farm boy and the Nazi, and so I closed my mind to him.

I saw these things quickly, for the officer was shouting again and the M.P.s, the prisoners a split second behind them, were facing left. They were facing the wall and the three posts in front of it, and then two M.P.s were leading each prisoner to a post, and the column was turning and marching back toward us, then turning back again to the wall and standing in two rows, twelve men to a row.

The prisoners, standing in front of the posts, looked very pale now. I looked at their thin fatigues and their bare hands. I wondered if the Westphalian felt the cold. I should have liked to have asked him.

Now, while the squad and the rest of us waited, two M.P.s walked to the post where the Westphalian stood, and there were strands of yellow, braided rope in their hands. You could see how new and clean the rope was, and when one of the M.P.s took a strand of rope and bent down at the post the other took the Westphalian by the shoulders and moved him back an inch or two. The first M.P. wrapped the rope around the Westphalian's ankles and around the post, and as he started to do this the Westphalian looked down, his hair falling forward, and he shuffled his feet back, watching until the M.P. was done. After that the second M.P. took the Westphalian's arms and put them back, one on each side, behind the post. Then the first M.P. tied them there, and the Westphalian, turning first to one side and then the other, watched intently.

He is trying to help them, I said to myself. Even now he is trying to do the right thing. I wondered how he could do this, and I knew he was brave because he was very afraid. I wondered how a man could be that brave, and then I saw a photographer, disobeying what the captain had told us, kneeling a few feet in front of the Westphalian, focusing his camera on him. I saw the Westphalian staring right back at the photographer, his eyes wide, his whole face questioning, and for that moment he seemed about to cry.

They left the Westphalian and went to the one in the middle, the one the captain had described as the Nazi. He already stood very stiffly against the post, and he did not move when they tied his feet. When they tied his arms behind his post he thrust them back there for them, and he squared his head and shoulders against the post. He was looking over the heads of all of us, and his face was very stern.

They went, then, to tie the third prisoner, the unimportant one. I looked at the other two, tied to the posts, looking out over the heads of the firing squad. I remembered the view of the valley behind my back. That is the last thing, I thought again, that the Westphalian will ever see. I looked at his long, pale face and I wondered if he was seeing anything. I knew that someone would think of him presently, as they might be thinking of him now, wondering what he was doing. I thought of a farmhouse, like so many we had passed in this war, the whitened stone cottage, the flat fields, an old woman, a turnip heap, and, somewhere in the yard, a dung pile.

They had finished tying the third prisoner. The three stood rigid against the posts like woodcuts of men facing execution. There were M.P. officers, clean and erect and efficient, moving between them, inspecting knots and saluting one another and then a chaplain—a full colonel, helmeted, wearing a trench coat but with a black satin stole around his neck and hanging down his front—stepped out from beside the squad and walked slowly, the small black book held in his hands in front of him, to the post where the Westphalian was tied.

I saw him say something to the Westphalian and I saw the Westphalian look to him and stare into his face and nod his head. I saw the chaplain reading from the book, and once I saw the Westphalian's lips moving, his head nodding a little, and then the chaplain was finished and the Westphalian was staring into his face as he moved away.

The chaplain stopped beside the one in the middle, the one described as the Nazi. The prisoner shook his head without looking at the chaplain, but the chaplain was saying something anyway, and then he moved on to the prisoner at the end who listened as the chaplain spoke.

When the chaplain had finished he walked back to a point behind the firing squad. Then two M.P.s stepped forward and walked to the Westphalian and one of them had in his hand a band of black cloth. He stood in back of the post and he reached around the head of the West-phalian to fix the cloth across his eyes.

This now, I said to myself, is that last moment that he will see anything on this earth. I wondered if the West-phalian was thinking that thought.

They fixed the bands over the eyes of the others. Then two M.P.s stepped forward and, starting with the prisoner on the left, pinned over the heart of each prisoner a white paper circle. The circles were about the size of a large orange. So they won't miss, I thought.

I was very cold, now, in these few gray seconds in this field. There was some saluting among the M.P. officers, and there were the three prisoners, each alone, their eyes bound with black and the white circles over their hearts, waiting.

I will not look, I was saying to myself. I think I am afraid to look. It is so easy to turn away, I thought, and then I said that I had come to see this when I did not have to because I had wanted to study myself.

I heard then the M.P. officer at the right of the firing squad give a command, and I saw the first row of twelve men drop to one knee. I heard another command and saw the rifles come up and I heard the sound of the stocks rustling against the clothing, and then I heard the Nazi in the middle shouting, guttural and loud in the morning, and I caught the end of his sentence.

". . . *Unser Fuehrer, Adolf Hitler!*"

At that moment—with the Nazi shouting—I heard the command to fire and I heard the explosion of the rifles, not quite all together and almost like a short burst from a machine gun. I was watching the Nazi, whose cry had drawn me at the last second, and I saw him stiffen in the noise and I saw the wall behind him chip and the dust come off it, and the Nazi flattened and rigid still against the post.

He's dead, I said to myself. They're all dead.

I looked, then, to the Westphalian, and as I looked I saw the blood on his front and I saw his head fall forward and then his shoulders and chest move out from the pole. I saw the Nazi standing rigid and the other prisoner beginning to sag out, and I was conscious again of the photographers. I remembered, now, seeing the one moving up to take pictures as they had prepared the prisoners, and now again he was kneeling in front of the Westphalian and shooting his camera at him and the others were moving about rapidly and shooting quickly, and I envied them their occupation.

I watched the weird dance, then, of the prisoners, dead but still dying. The Nazi stood firm against the post, only his head bent forward, but the one on the left sagged forward slowly, and then I saw the Westphalian go, first to his left and then, pausing, to his right, swaying. I saw him hang there for a moment, and then I saw him pitch forward, hung by his wrists, bent in the middle, his head down to his knees, his long hair hanging, the whole of him straining at the ropes around his wrists.

He's not alive, I said to myself. He's really dead.

Two medics walked up to him then and the one, bending down, looked into his eyes and, with his fingers, closed the lids. Then the second, bending down, slid his hands under the Westphalian's armpits, lifting him so that the first could put a stethoscope to his chest. In a moment they dropped him, leaving him sagging and swaying a little, and they moved on to the Nazi in the middle.

The Nazi strained a little at the ropes but his body was still rigid. I saw them pausing longer at the Nazi, the two of them looking at him more carefully. I was wondering if they were really finding the Nazi harder to kill. They stood there, talking to each other, putting the stethoscope on him for the second time, and then they finally moved on. They found the other prisoner dead and they walked back to the group beside the firing squad. They saluted the officer in charge and I heard the officer's command to the squad and saw the squad, facing left, march back across the field and up the path.

"What he said," one of the Ninth Army men was saying, "means 'Long live our Fuehrer, Adolf Hitler.'"

We waited for the photographers to finish taking their pictures of the prisoners in their positions of death and of the two M.P.s cutting them from the poles. They cut the Westphalian down first and put him on a stretcher, and then two others came with a white mattress cover and they slid him, feet first, off the stretcher and into the mattress cover. They left the mattress cover in front of the post and they went on to the Nazi.

When the M.P.s were finished and we were ready to leave I looked for the last time at what was left. There was the wall, chipped behind each post, and among the marks the bullets had made were small splashes of blood. There were the three posts, spattered, and before each post a white mattress cover, filled with a body. There were the stretchers, blood-spattered, and on the frozen ground were strewn the things typically American—the black paper ends from the film packs, the flash bulbs, milky-white and expended, and an empty, crumpled Lucky Strike cigarette package. An M.P., a rifle on his shoulder, walked up and down.

We went back to the small office near the gate. Our fingers and hands were stiff and ached from the cold, and we stood near the potbellied stove. There was a G.I. working at a filing cabinet near the stove and he started to talk to us.

"I'm glad it's over," he said.

"I am, too," I said.

"Not as much as us," he said. "For three days this place has been on end. We haven't been able to get anything else done."

The captain who had led us to the field came in. I thanked him and told him I thought it had all gone very well.

"We should have used combat troops," he said. "This bunch was so nervous that—just between us—there were only three bullets in one of the bull's-eyes, only three out of eight."

"Maybe one had the blank," I said. "That would be three out of seven."

"I don't know," the captain said. "I don't know if they used one blank."

The chaplain who had pronounced the last rites came in. He stood talking with another officer who was, I judged, the chaplain attached to the M.P. battalion.

"Well," he said, sticking out his hand, "I think it was conducted very well."

"Thank you," the other said, taking his hand. "Come and see us again. We hope next time it will be under more pleasant circumstances."

We went out and found our driver and he wanted to know how it was. We said it was all right, and we drove back. By afternoon the weather had cleared and the Germans came over. They came in so low that I could see the black crosses on the first plane and they bombed the hell out of us. They killed Jack Frankish and three Belgians, and Colonel Flynn Andrew died later in the hospital.

Damn, I said to myself, I wish this war were over and I wish I were home. For such a long time in September we had all thought we might be home for Christmas.

Excerpt from *Transition*

(Autumn 1945)

from *Once They Heard the Cheers*

Those were the good years, right after the war. I mean that if you got out of it alive and all in one piece, and if you did not lose anyone close to you, and if you had done honest work during that time, no matter what it was or where it was, you knew that the next years, after all that had happened, had to be the good ones, as long as your luck held out.

It was early in the fall after the war ended, and I was standing in the sports department by Wilbur Wood's desk. Wilbur Wood was the sports editor of the paper, and before that he had been its boxing writer. He was rather large-boned and balding, and because at some time his nose had been hit he looked tough, but he was a soft and sentimental man. During the war he used to write me V-mail letters, giving me the gossip of the office and recounting something that he had found memorable or amusing in sports. Once he described a block that Doc Blanchard, the Army fullback, had thrown in the Yankee Stadium on Tree Adams, a 6-foot, 7-inch

Notre Dame tackle. I can still see it the way Wilbur described it in the letter—which I got after we had crossed
the border into Germany—with Adams going up in the
air and turning a somersault and landing on his head. In
all his letters Wilbur said he liked what I was writing,
and several times he added that he guessed now he
would never be able to get me into sports.

I had been wanting to get into sports since I had been
in high school, and trying, with time out for the war, for
the eight years I had been on the paper. In high school I
weighed 118 pounds, and my heroes were the football
players, the ones whom 10,000 came out to see in a big
game, filling the concrete stands and, across the field, the
wooden bleachers, and lining the sidelines. Several of
them were six feet tall, or more, and must have weighed
180 or 190 pounds, and I felt that I was fortunate when I
was in the same class with one or another of them.

I would sit near the back of the room, so that I could
watch them in their letter sweaters lolling behind the
desks, their legs out into the aisle. They made their desks
seem small, and the books seemed small in their hands, and
at the end of the class, when we all stood up and walked
out, they towered not only above the rest of us but above
the teacher. They seemed to me to be men, and as we all
walked out of the class I felt that they could walk right out
of the school and be men out there in the world too.

Many years later, when I came to live in training camp
and travel with the New York Football Giants and then
the Green Bay Packers in their great years, they still
seemed big to me, those heroes of my youth. Remembering them, in a Giant or a Packer dressing room, I still had
to tell myself that Tommy Mallon and Eddie Williams
and Ernie Jansen had been only teen-agers, really, and
that they were never such superb football players as Andy
Robustelli or Alex Webster or Frank Gifford, with the

Giants, or Bart Starr, Paul Hornung, Jimmy Taylor, Forrest Gregg, Jerry Kramer, or Willie Davis of the Packers.

That was how bad I had it in high school, when I was too frail for football and afraid of a baseball thrown near the head and had been a reluctant starter and worse finisher in street fights. Once, when we were both eight years old, they put the shoemaker's son and me together in the school playground with gloves on us, and he punched me around for three one-minute rounds.

"You know," I said, a long time after that, to Sugar Ray Robinson, the greatest fighter I ever saw, "you and I fought the same guy. When we were little kids he punched my head off in a playground fight."

"Who was that?" Robinson said.

"Vic Troisi," I said.

"Vic Troisi?" Robinson said. "Did I fight him?"

"Yes," I said, "you fought him in the Eastern Parkway, and knocked him out in the first round.

"Is that so?" Robinson said.

It was the same with Frank Boucher, another hero of my youth, when he centered a great forward line of the New York Rangers, with the Cook brothers, Bill at right wing and Bun on the left, and they won the Stanley Cup twice. The year after the war ended, Boucher was coaching the Rangers, and he and I got on the subway at the Garden to ride out to Brooklyn, where the team was to practice, and I told him about a remembered youthful embarrassment that I still carried with me after thirteen years.

"In high school," I said, as we sat together on the subway, "I played on the hockey team. We were a terrible team. We won one game and tied one in two years, and one night we played between the periods of a Bronx Tigers game in the Bronx Coliseum. You were refereeing, and in one scramble after a face-off I knocked you down."

Turned toward him, I was watching Boucher's face. I was waiting for some sign of recollection to invade it, to start with a quickening in the eyes and then around them, but nothing was happening.

"When I knocked you down," I said, "the crowd roared, and I wanted to melt into the ice, because I was so ashamed that I had knocked Frank Boucher down, and people were laughing. Do you remember me knocking you down?"

"No," Boucher said, smiling now but shaking his head. "In fact, I don't even remember refereeing that game."

There was no way I could ever be one of them—first the football heroes of high school and then, as I projected myself into manhood, those paragons of the professional sports. When I read the sports pages, though, I discovered that the sportswriters rode on the same trains and lived in the same hotels with the ballplayers and visited the training camps of the prize fighters and knew them man to man. Now the sportswriters acquired an eminence of their own by association with those whom, if my mother had known anything about sports, she would have referred to as "the higher ups." If you were a German-American family that had survived World War I in this country, when they called sauerkraut "Liberty Cabbage" and changed the name of Wittenberg Place in the Bronx to Bradley Avenue, and if you were not of that arrogant type that had always made trouble for themselves and the world, then you were so humble that all you hoped for your offspring was that he would get a steady job on which he would come to know those who hired and fired.

"He has a very good job," my mother said once, after I had started on the paper and she was telling me about one of my former high school classmates. "He works for the telephone company."

"What does he do?" I asked, wondering if he climbed poles or sat in an office half the size of a gymnasium with half a hundred others, all of them at desks, all of them poring over open ledgers.

"I don't know," she said, "but he's getting to know the higher-ups."

They do not run newspapers the way they run ball clubs, though, because there is a paternalism that contravenes their professionalism. There is no place to trade off old baseball writers who can no longer go into the hole or get the bat around in time to meet the fast ball, and so they go on beyond their best days, while their replacements wait in vain to get into the lineup. For two years after college I ran copy, and when I was twenty-four they were still calling me "Boy." For the next four years, before they sent me to report the war, I covered and wrote almost everything from push-cart fires on the Lower East Side to political campaigns, but when I came back from the war I figured I finally had the leverage to get into sports.

We were in Weimar, the birthplace of the Republic that had failed, and it must have been about seven o'clock when I was awakened that morning by a rooster crowing. They had us in two small hotels, and the sun was coming into the room, bright on the flowered rug, and I lay in bed and looked out the open window into the May morning. I could see treetops, the new leaves yellow-green and clean, and through them housetops. I could hear Germans talking and working in the yard below, and I lay in the soft bed between the clean sheets and for the first time in a long time I was empty of fear. On the morning that peace came again to Europe I lay in that bed and it came to me that all of the rest of my life, for however long it would go on, would derive from this morning.

Some years later I asked the oldest son of a Massachusetts shoe worker what it had been like for him when he had awakened in that hotel room in Philadelphia on what must have been his own great and beginning morning. The night before, in the thirteenth round of one of the most vicious of heavyweight title fights, Rocky Marciano had knocked out Jersey Joe Walcott with a single right hand.

"You know how it is when you wake up in a strange place and you don't know where you are?" Marciano said. "I thought to myself, 'Something nice happened to me.' Then I remembered, 'That's right. Last night I won the heavyweight championship of the world.'"

We had the best duty in the war, those of us who by the accidents of age and occupation were picked to report it. The Army provided our transportation and our keep, and we who otherwise might have been carrying rifles and sleeping in foxholes, carried typewriters and slept under roofs even as we pursued our profession. We saluted no one physically, and figuratively only those we felt deserved it. We never had that responsibility that came down from generals to noncoms of sending others where they knew some of them would be killed and others maimed, and so we would never have to live with that for the rest of our lives. Our only responsibility was to order ourselves to go where we could see it, and then to try to tell it as it really was, as those who were being killed and maimed would have wanted to tell it if they could, and not as some of the big-name writers wrote it, or told it on lecture tours, after they came back from junkets on which they were briefed at any Army headquarters or maybe even at some Division command post.

"It was a marvelous speech," Harry Markson was telling me some months after I came back. "You should have heard it."

We had had lunch at Lindy's and were walking west on 50th Street back to Madison Square Garden. Harry was doing publicity then for Mike Jacobs when Jacobs was running boxing in this country, and later Harry would run the boxing at the Garden.

"You know he was a big Roosevelt man," Harry was saying, talking about the writer, "and this was at a Democratic fund-raising luncheon at the Waldorf. I'll never forget it because at one point he said, 'And when your son, your brother, or your husband lands on that foreign beach under fire, and when he finally finds a moment of respite from the shelling and the horror and opens his K-ration, do you know what he finds therein? Among the other things, he finds four cigarettes. Now someone must have thought of those cigarettes. Could it have been F.D.R.?'"

What I said I don't want in this book, and then I said, "If he'd ever landed on a beach or made an attack and opened a K-ration during his moment of respite, he'd have found that the cigarettes were Avalons or Wings, and he wouldn't have mentioned them."

You see, if they didn't get the cigarettes right they weren't going to get any of it really right for the sons and the brothers and the husbands, and for all those who also served by waiting. We despised them while they were doing it, and there was one of us, who tended to be irascible anyway, who became absolutely irate one night when he read in a letter from his wife that she had spent $3.00 to listen to a lecture by one of them who had been with us for five days, and that she had found what he had said fascinating. After it was over though, and I was introduced to the cigarette shill, he was so impressed by a magazine piece I had written about Rocky Graziano and so humble and obviously ashamed of all his own work that, reasoning that it was too late to do any good, anyway, I found that I didn't have the heart to level on him.

So we knew that the cigarettes were in the same breakfast issue with the insipid port-and-egg-yolk, and we learned the mechanics of how war was made on the ground, how attacks were mounted, and how men behaved under stress and great danger—and what they did and how they did it and why. We learned early, of course, the rules of self-preservation, how to analyze a situation map in order to decide where to go and where not to go, and our ears became attuned to the sounds of shelling, the difference between the incoming and the outgoing, so that we were not constantly cowering. When, in late afternoon we would come back from the front on a day when we had really been out, and not just covering something from the perimeter around regiment or battalion, we would be joyous in the jeep, sometimes even singing, so exalted were we to be still alive.

"What's the matter with you?" John Groth said to me one evening. He had come into my room where I had been trying for more than an hour to write my piece about what I had seen that day. He was doing his drawing and his watercolors then for the Marshall Field publications, and two years later I would take him into Stillman's Gym for the first time and then introduce him to the baseball and thoroughbred-racing people, and he would do those fine things he did on sports.

"The matter?" I said.

"You look terrible," he said. "What's going on?"

"I'm coming apart," I said.

It was late September, and we were inside Germany now. That day several of us had gone up to the Ninth Infantry Division, and a captain named Lindsey Nelson had taken us up to a battalion command post in the Huertgen Forest. Nineteen years later I was driving north out of Manhattan one night, and when I got on the Major Deegan Expressway in the Bronx, I could see, across the Harlem River, the lights of the Polo Grounds. That was after the Giants had gone to San Francisco and the Mets had moved in, and I turned on the car radio and I heard Lindsey doing the game.

There were two hundred square miles of it in the Huertgen, the fir trees sixty feet tall and planted ten feet apart in absolutely straight rows. It was a picture forest, and there in the cool, soft, and shaded dampness, in a place that had once known the cathedral quiet that is a forest's own, they were dying between the trees and among the ferns.

"I don't think I can do it any more," I said to John.

"You have to," he said.

"Day after day," I said, "I see those kids going out and sacrificing themselves. They haven't even had a chance to live yet. They're eighteen and nineteen and twenty, and they're giving their lives, and what am I doing for them? They deserve the best writers we have, and except for Hemingway, they're not here."

John had just come back from living for several days with Heminway in a house he had taken over in the Siegfried Line. They had become friends, and later John would illustrate the Living Library edition of *Men Without Women*.

"I try," I said, "but it isn't any good."

"You can't write *War and Peace* every night," John said. "Nobody can."

"I'm not trying to," I said. "I'm just trying to get it right, but I can get so little of it in."

"Just do the best you can for today," John said, "and tomorrow try again."

"And then every afternoon," I said, "we wave them a hearty farewell, and we leave them up there. We run around with our little notebooks and pencils making a living, and then come back here and leave them to die up there."

"Gee," John said, "you've got it bad. I don't know."

"I don't know, either," I said. "The whole thing is wrong."

"I mean I don't know about you," John said. "You'd better pull yourself together. You know what's going to happen to you if you don't pull yourself together?"

"Who knows?" I said.

"I know," John said. "They'll come around and wrap you up and send you home."

"I'm no psycho," I said.

"You will be if you don't pull yourself together," John said. "You want to be sent home? Then you better stop this. You better just write your piece for today and say to yourself, 'That's that for today and there's another day tomorrow.'"

"There isn't for a lot of them," I said.

"You've got to do that," John said. "You really have to do that."

We talked for another half hour or so, and then John left, telling me again to just take it one day at a time, and I finished my piece, such as it was. It was about how the Germans had all the main roads, and all the crossroads in the forest zeroed in for their artillery, and about how they had the pillboxes hidden among the trees and about the land mines that would explode at knee height and take a man's legs and his masculinity and about the almost invisible trip wires they had strung from tree to tree so that, when they were touched, they would set off a whole chain of explosives.

When I finished I took the piece across the street to where the censors were set up, and I handed it to one of them and I came back and went to bed. I was fortunate that night because there was no way I could have known then that it would take more than three months to get the Germans out of what remained of that forest, and that five infantry divisions and parts of four others would be chewed up and we would suffer 33,000 casualties in there. I was fortunate, too, that I had John Groth for a friend and that he scared me about being sent home, and I lay in bed that night thinking about that and about how odd it was that he should be fathering me because we were always fathering John.

John was the most impressionable of all of us, and he saw everything through the wide, unspoiled eyes of a child. He knew little about the martial art, about troop dispositions or unit actions, and when, now and then, the others of us would get into an argument about where we were going, John would never put in but just come along.

"Wherever you guys are going," he'd say, "it's all right with me."

When we got up to where we were going, and the rest of us were trying to cover our ignorance with professional poses, the way insecure outsiders do when they want to seem to belong, John would ask the simple civilian questions that were the best, but that gave the impression that he had no idea of what was going on.

"But I don't understand," John would ask some major or captain who was filling us in. "Why are you fellows going to do that?"

It was the same two years later, when I took him to Stillman's Gym the first time. After I introduced him to Lou Stillman, I left him standing behind the two rings on the main floor while I went back to the dressing rooms to interview some fighter, probably one who would be fighting in the Garden that Friday night. When I came back out a half hour or so later, John was still standing there and sketching, with the fighters shadowboxing around him and sparring in the raised rings above him.

"How are you doing?" I said.

"I don't know," he said, showing me his notebook and riffling through the pages.

"Hold it a second," I said. "Go back a couple of pages. There. That's Rocky Graziano's right leg, isn't it?"

Graziano toed in with his right foot, and his right leg was slightly bowed. I always figured that that was one of the reasons he was such a great right-hand puncher, and now, with a few quickly scrawled lines on a notebook page, John had captured with absolute definition the one leg that was distinctively different from all the other legs in that gym.

"Who's Graziano?" John said.

"He's the leading contender for the middleweight title," I said. "He's the hottest fighter in years."

"Gee," John. "He is?"

"Yes," I said, "and he's the reason most of this crowd is here in those chairs and up in the balcony."

"Oh," John said, and then pointing, "it's that fella over there."

"Right," I said. "That's Rocky Graziano."

The next week, when I stopped off at the gym again, Lou Stillman spotted me as I came in. He hollered at me and motioned for me to come over to where he was sitting on the high stool under the time clock and from where he ran the traffic in and out of the two rings.

"Listen," he said, growling at me in what someone once described in print as that ash-can voice, which Lou resented. "You know that beard you brought in here last week?"

"John Groth?" I said.

"Yeah," Lou said. "You know what he done? Two days later he come in here with a whole gang of beards."

"He teaches at the Art Students' League," I said.

"Up on my balcony there's a whole gang of beards, all of them drawin'," Lou said. "What are they tryin' to turn this place into, anyway?"

"I don't know," I said. "Ask them."

"You ask them," Lou said. "I ain't got time to bother with them."

The next time I saw John, I told him what Stillman had said. I told him that Stillman had all the fighters cowed, which was the way he kept order in the gym full of them, and I said that some of that carried over to the way he talked to everyone.

"Oh, we get along fine," John said. "You know what Stillman does at home on Sundays? He paints in oil, and we talk about that."

"There are some fighters I know," I said, "who won't believe it."

Lying in that bed, though, that night after John had fathered me, I remembered the time he showed up without his bedroll and slept in my trench coat. I remembered the time I had found him in a barn behind a chateau in France, drawing in ink with a goose quill. The dampness had affected his drawing paper, so that he couldn't get the lines he wanted with his pens, and he had run down a goose and plucked a couple of quills and sharpened them with a penknife.

"Now I can draw thin lines, thick lines, any kind of lines I want," he said, "but with everything that's going on over here, I don't get enough chance to draw the lines."

There was the time, too, when he was worried that he was going to lose his accreditation because he was supposed to be back at Army Group instead of up with us. Then I remembered the day he was so obviously depressed that I asked him what was wrong, and he showed me the letter he had just received from a friend back home in New York.

"I play volleyball for the Grand Central Y," John said, "and this guy is on the team, too. He writes here, see, that they got into the semifinals of the Nationals at Kansas City, and look at this."

With his index finger he pointed out the sentence ending one paragraph: "Al Burwinkle says that if you had been
with us we would have won the national championship."

"He's got to be kidding," I said.

"No he's not," John said. "Al Burwinkle is our captain,
and if he says we could have won it if I was there, we
could have won it."

"Those guys must be on another planet," I said.
"They're playing volleyball in Kansas City and you're
covering a war in Germany, and they're blaming you because they lost?"

"That's what Al Burwinkle said," John said, and he
walked away still depressed.

So each day after the night John scared me about being sent home, I would tell myself that I would just try to
do the best I could for that day, and then hope I could
get more of it in, and right, the next day. I always lived,
though, as most of us did, with that suppressed guilt
about the way it was at the front and the way we had it,
and with that growing personal fear. Man is born with
the illusion that he is immortal, and as every good writer
who has gone into man's reactions in war has written, he
goes under fire the first time shielded by that illusion
and believing that others will be killed but that it will not
happen to him. Then it happens, not to him, but so close
to him that it could have been to him, and that is the beginning of the fear.

"A good soldier does not worry," Hemingway wrote in
his introduction to *Men at War*, the anthology he edited.
"He knows that nothing happens until it actually happens, and you live your life up until then. Danger only
exists at the moment of danger. To live properly in war,
the individual eliminates all such things as potential danger. Then a thing is only bad when it is bad. It is neither
bad before nor after. Cowardice, as distinguished from

panic, is almost always simply a lack of ability to suspend the functioning of the imagination. Learning to suspend your imagination and live completely in the very second of the present minute with no before and no after is the greatest gift a soldier can acquire. It, naturally, is the opposite of all those gifts a writer should have."

That was the problem we had, we who were not soldiers but writers, we who were not ordered by others but had to order ourselves. Each day, two or three to a jeep and with a G.I. driver from the motor pool, we would go up toward the front and stop off at Corps to be briefed on what the divisions were doing, and then we would split up by jeeps and go to one division or another. At Division they would fill us in about what the regiments were doing, and at Regiment what the battalions were doing. Then we would go up to a battalion and sometimes to a company or a platoon until we got what we thought were our stories.

At first, and functioning behind that illusion of immortality, we all bore ourselves as if we were brave, but then, depending upon what happened around us, and to us, and upon our separate abilities to suspend our imaginations, we all came to live in fear. Then it became more difficult to go beyond battalion, and we went less often, and there wasn't a one of us who lived through it who could honestly say to himself that he had covered the war the way he should have. Two I knew, who had been in it too long and whose pieces had become irrational, were called home, and I heard later that, months after it was over, one of them was still walking around New York in uniform and carrying his musette bag. Then, when the Germans broke through during the Bulge, scattering our troops and us in panic, several of us, including the one who had been so irate about his wife buying that lecture by the Five Day Wonder, took off for Paris and London, and the rest understood. When their

replacements arrived, we watched them sally forth behind the shields of their own illusions, as we once had,
and then always that thing happened, whatever it was,
near them and thus to them, and they too became, like
us, cautious in their fear.

The soldier fights the enemy and his fear, and exercises
that fear, if it is not so big that he can't handle it, against
the person of the enemy. For the writer, implanted
weaponless in war, his two personal enemies are his guilt
and his fear, and after a while it was only our guilt that
sent us out against our fear. We did whatever we did because, knowing what those we left at the front were doing,
we were ashamed not to, and if we were honest with ourselves, we knew that all we were doing was trying not just
to go on living, but to go on living with ourselves.

If ever there is a time to die in a war, it is not after the
issue has been decided. That time came after the bridge
across the Rhine was captured at Remagen, and we broke
out of the bridgehead on the east bank, and one day, five
years later, I was sitting in the Yankee dugout at the Stadium watching batting practice, and talking with Ralph
Houk. This was when Houk was a second-string catcher
with the Yankees and, of course, before he managed them
and later the Detroit Tigers, and I knew what he had done
in the war. Among other things, during the Bulge he had
taken a night patrol in to Bastogne while the Germans
had it surrounded, and he had brought out the plans for
the defense of the town. During the last week of the 1949
baseball season, though, with the Yankees and the Red
Sox wrestling for the pennant in a game at the Stadium,
Johnny Pesky had slid home under Houk's tag with the
winning run. The next day, all of the New York newspapers, and I suppose the Boston papers as well, carried a
photo sequence of the play intended to let the reader
make up his own mind as to whether Pesky had been safe

or out, and now a lot of people finally knew Houk's name because an umpire had said he had missed a tag in a game.

"You remember Remagen?" Houk was saying in the dugout. We had been talking about the war that had just started in Korea, and Houk had said that he couldn't tell much about it from what he read in the paper, and that got him onto our war.

"Remagen?" I said. "Sure I remember it."

"You remember," Houk said, "how, in the town, there was one road that turned right along the river?"

"I know where you mean," I said. "One day I came back across the river and I was driving along our side, and somebody was working south along the other side. You know the river's nowhere near as wide there as the Hudson, and I could see and hear a firefight going on over there in the trees just south of the bridge."

"You saw that?" Houk said, looking right at me.

"Yes."

"That was me," Houk said. "We had a hell of a fire-fight there. I'll be damned."

"So will I," I said, sitting there and watching Joe DiMaggio, Yogi Berra, Phil Rizzuto, Hank Bauer, and the others taking their batting practice.

Once they broke out of that bridgehead, though, and the tanks started east, the infantry rode on the tanks or in trucks for miles before they had to dismount, cursing, to clear out the scattered pockets of resistance. Now it was obvious that the Germans were finally beaten, and now the dying seemed sadder than ever. In the residential suburbs of Halle, the birthplace of Handel, they fell among the fallen petals of magnolias, when there was no longer any reason for it. Now the fear, suppressed for so long, of not surviving swept the troops themselves, whole units, and we were all of us one as the time wore down slowly to that new morning.

As I lay in that bed now, on that morning, free again at last, I heard the voices of the Germans in the yard below rising and, although I had no idea what they were saying, I could tell that they were arguing, women's voices among men's. Then the voices of two men began to dominate, as if they had singled out each other, and I thought that maybe this would turn into a fist fight, and I would enjoy seeing Germans fighting among themselves. When I got up and looked down, though, I couldn't see them through the leaves and branches of the trees, and even as I tried to make them out, the intervals between the verbal exchanges became longer and the two voices less assertive, so I went across the hall and washed and shaved. When I came back there were no sounds at all in the yard below, and I dressed and went downstairs and walked, in the cool, clear morning, around the corner to the other hotel where they fed us. We sat there, eating and then smoking with our coffee, and we were all of us loose and lazy and dull, like men who have slept themselves out for the first time in a long while.

Several of us walked back to our hotel together. We got a jeep and a driver from the motor pool, and we drove out of Weimar into the Thuringian countryside. The lilacs were blooming in the farmyards, and under the yellow of the morning sun the apple trees were white and pink along the sides of the roads. In the rich brown fields the Germans were walking along the furrows, sowing their grain, and we went out to get a story of V-E Day in Germany because it would be the last story and it was a way to end a job.

We drove around for almost an hour, following our map and looking for the Third Armored Division, until we saw the tanks in a field on the left. There were four or five divisions that we had come to know well and for whom we had the highest admiration. The Third Armored was one, and so we had decided that we would end the war with them—or what was left of them.

There were seventeen of the tanks parked in the field on the left and along the partial cover of a long gray barn. Across the road on the right the land rose, and on the flat of the rise and forming a quadrangle there were some low, brown wooden barracks of what had been a Nazi youth camp. We could see the tankers walking about and lolling in the sun on the plot of winter-browned grass in the middle of the quadrangle, so we drove up the rise and into the quadrangle.

The lieutenant was the eighth commanding officer the company had had in ten months of fighting, which will give you an idea of what they had been through, and he had the Silver Star and the Bronze Star and the Purple Heart with cluster. His name was Thomas Cooper and he was from Henderson, Kentucky, and we asked him how I Company of the First Battalion of the Thirty-third Regiment of the Third Armored Division had heard the news of the German surrender.

"I got a telephone call from Battalion headquarters at 9:10 last night," he said. "I told the first sergeant. He had an old nickel-plated horn from a Kraut car, and he went to the door and blew the horn a couple of times. Then he hollered, 'The war is over. The war is over, you guys. It's official now.'"

"Then what happened?" one of us said.

"Nothing much," the lieutenant said. "We knew for a long time it was gonna be over."

Some of the kids from the company were standing around us as we talked with the lieutenant. Out of the eighty-five who had started out with the I Company in Normandy, there were only six originals left on the day that peace came, and one of the best was a staff sergeant named Juan Haines from Gatesville, Texas.

"This tank of yours," I said to Haines. "What's its name?"

At the beginning, almost all of them gave their tanks names. I wanted to find out if the soldier who went through the war with a tank had any affection for it, if he felt anything about his tank on the day the war ended.

"I don't rightly know," Haines said. "This is the fourth tank we had. We lost three."

"When did your tank fire its last shot?" another of us asked, trying to establish when the war in Europe had really ended for the sergeant and the others in his tank.

"I'll have to think," Haines said.

He was tall and thin and with reddish hair. He stood looking at the ground at his feet.

"It was on the outskirts of Dessau a week or so ago," he said.

"It was April 22," one of the other kids, listening said. "We were firing on a pillbox."

"Was the pillbox built against a building," I asked him, "or was it out in the open?"

"It was out in the open," the kid said, "covering a field."

"Did you get the pillbox?"

"Hell, we got 'em all," one of the other kids said.

We turned back to the lieutenant. He had been standing and listening, a little bored by our questions.

"What will you people do now?" I said. "After all, it's V-E Day, and are you going to do anything special?"

"Well," the lieutenant said, "at noon we're going to drink a toast to General Eisenhower. He sent the division champagne after we crossed the Rhine, and there's enough for one glass for each man."

"Then what?"

"We have a ball game on this afternoon," the lieutenant said, "and there's some German museum near here, and one of the platoons will visit that."

We walked around with the lieutenant for a while, looking in at the kids in the barracks. Most of them were lying on their bunks in the barracks, brown uniforms on the brown Army blankets, reading or writing letters, and when we stopped to talk with them they wanted to know if we knew where they were going next, and if they could get home soon. It was strange, having them ask us the questions, and there was one who wanted me to put his lieutenant's name in the paper. He said his lieutenant's name was Loren Cantrell and that the lieutenant came from Springfield, Illinois, and that the kids under him wanted to get him a citation.

We got back into the jeep, and as we started to drive out of the quadrangle we could hear a guitar being played, and we could hear the voice of a G.I. singing. The G.I. was singing that song they retitled, "Those Eighty-eights Are Breaking up that Old Gang of Mine."

They had been a great outfit, the Third Armored, and suddenly in one day they weren't anything that was important any more. Riding along, I thought about how great they had been at Mons where, with the First Infantry Division, "The Big Red One" that had been in it since Africa, they cut off the Germans trying to get back to the Siegfried Line and killed nobody knew how many and took 8,000 prisoners, including three generals. On the day we crossed the German border with them and they took Roetgen, they were the first to capture a German town since Napoleon, and when they breached the Siegfried Line and were pinned down by the shelling on a hillside outside of Stolberg, their general came up, erect, immaculate and handsome, and got them out of their holes and up the hill.

I remembered them, with their tanks painted white, in the snow and fog of the Ardennes, and then driving across the brown-gray Cologne plain in the mist and the rain and then taking the city, fighting around the cathedral and knocking out a German tank at the cathedral steps. After they broke out of the bridgehead across the Rhine, I was with them the day they went more than ninety miles behind the German lines. It was the longest single combat advance in the world's military history, and the next evening, in the dusk and on a dirt road outside of Paderborn, their general was killed.

"It can't be him," the young lieutenant said. "I'm sure it ain't him."

"They've identified the body," the major said.

"I sure hope it ain't him," the lieutenant said.

We had spent the night where they had coiled the tanks and half-tracks in a field next to a woods. It was eight o'clock in the morning, and I was standing, talking with some tankers around a fire, when the major called me over and the colonel told us that they had found the general's body. We got our typewriters out of the jeeps and we walked over to a fieldstone farmhouse and we wrote our pieces. I wrote about what the young lieutenant said, and why at first he couldn't believe it, and about the risks the general had always taken and how, two nights before, he had called us over to his CP to tell us that at six o'clock the next morning we would be starting that drive to the north that took us more than ninety miles.

"This thing is almost over now," one of us had said. "When it is, what are you going to do?"

"I have a son," the general had said. "He's four years old now, and I don't know him. We're going to get acquainted, and that's going to take a lot of time."

Now, in the stone farmhouse, we finished our pieces about the death of the general, and they gave us an armed jeep to escort us back around the pockets of Germans who were still holding out. In places on the way back we left the roads and drove across fields and over low hills, following the tracks the tanks and the half-tracks had made, and when we got to Marburg we found the press camp set up in a big private mansion on a hill. We turned our pieces in to the censors, and then gave the rest of them the word that Major General Maurice Rose was dead.

"He was a Jew, wasn't he?" one of them asked me.

"A Jew?" I said. "How would I know? All I know is that he was a great general, and he's dead."

We learned later that he was the son of a Denver rabbi, and that a congressman from Colorado—so far from it all—had stood up in the House of Representatives and made an impassioned speech calling for a Congressional investigation into the general's death. To me he was a great general, as two years later, when Jackie Robinson came up to the major leagues, he was a great ballplayer. It should have been as simple as that, and after the general was killed, the Third Armored linked up with the Second Armored, coming down from the north, and they sealed off the Ruhr pocket with 374,000 German prisoners inside.

So we left them now to have their one drink of warm champagne in their tin cups and to their ball game and the visit to the museum, and we drove back between the same brown fields, with the Germans still working in them, and through the same little towns we had passed through coming out. In all of the towns there were duck ponds, and there were white ducks and geese and small yellow goslings paddling around in them. There were young German women wheeling their babies in the sun, and there were other women and children waiting patiently near the doorsteps of their small stone and stuccoed houses. They were waiting for the American trucks to come through, loaded with the German soldiers on the way back to the prison cages.

In one town we stopped to let the trucks go by. The American trucks came through the town quickly, fast and high and with the dust rising around them and behind them, and with the grinding of their gearing and the noise of their exhaust loud in the tight aisle of the road lined by the small closely packed houses. Ahead of the convoy the women and children had spread, jumping into their doorways as the trucks passed through at high speed, each truck, after the first, fifteen feet behind the one ahead.

In the open trucks the prisoners stood tightly, seventy packed into each half-ton truck. They stood facing the rear, their gray-green uniforms dirty and dust-covered, all of them rocking together with the motion of the trucks, the rush of air from the forward motion blowing at the backs of their heads.

From some of the doorways the women and children threw bread. Some of the men in the trucks managed to catch some of the hard half-loaves, but more often the bread bounced off their hands or bodies or hit the sides of the trucks and then rolled in the dust under the trucks that followed. The women and children who threw no bread just stood, their heads turning back and forth in the doorways, as they tried to recognize in a second in the seas of faces on the trucks someone of whom they had not heard for many months, because they wanted to know if he was still alive now that peace had come to Europe again.

When we got back to the hotel we went into the press-room and wrote our last stories. We wrote them quickly, just telling what it was like where we were on V-E Day in Germany and not trying to tell everything that we wished we could tell. For the last time we turned our stories over to the censors, and then we had lunch. After lunch I went back into the pressroom, and I wrote a cable to Edmond Bartnett, who was my boss on the *Sun*. The cable said: "Hopefully request permission start homeward shortly." That night I got the answer back: "Gladly grant permission for homeward trip. Bartnett."

We had written so hard every day for so long that it was a strange feeling. We did not know how to kill time. We just sat around a lot and talked some about the best moments, but mostly about our homes and our families and about what we might do now. I said that I had wanted to write sports ever since I had been in high school, and the irate one, who had taken off for London during the Bulge but had joined us again for the easier going after the Rhine crossing, said that he had already done that. He said that he had had enough of games and, as he put it, "the spoiled brats who play them." Then one night the word came.

The next morning we walked across the street under the trees with our blankets and our helmets and our canteens and our mess gear, and we turned them in to a lieutenant behind a table set up just inside the doorway of a small one-family house. He gave us our slips of paper for them, and they put us in a weapons carrier, and we rode out to the small airfield on the top of the raised ground.

While we waited for the C-47 to come in, we stood in the shade under the wing of another plane. There was a major there, and he had with him a young pilot in a leather jacket and dark green dress trousers.

"This man has a hell of a story," the major said to me. "You should write it."

The young pilot told me his story, standing in the shade under the wing of the plane. He said he had been shot down over the outskirts of Berlin, and when he parachuted down he landed in the walled garden of a large estate. As he came down in the garden, the S.S. guards grabbed him and took him into the big stone mansion.

"I was standing in the living room," he said. "It was a great big room with a lot of rich furnishing and oil paintings, when the door opens and the big shot walks in. Who the hell is it but Herman Goering, himself. I recognized him right away from his pictures—a big fat guy with medals."

The young flier said that Goering treated him very well. He said Goering knew a lot about American planes, and then he told me how he was liberated by the Russians, and I told him it was a good story.

"Are you going to write it?" he said. "What paper will it be in?"

"No," I said. "I'm sorry. The war is over. Two months ago it would have been a real good story, and two weeks ago it would still have been a good story. Now I think it's still a good story, but the war here is over, and the day it ended the people stopped wanting to read these stories from here. My own head is filled with good stories, but no one would print them now. I'm sorry about it."

I don't think the young pilot quite understood why I would not write his story. He flew back in the plane to Paris with us, and I noticed that he was watching Victor Bernstein, who was sitting across from him and who had his typewriter on his lap, trying to write a story.

Victor Bernstein came over late, not really to write about the fighting but to write about post-war Europe. He wrote some of the fighting, but now he was doing what he was meant to do, and I realized this as I watched him typing on his knees until the motion of the plane and his concentration on the lines of his typing became too much for him. Then he put the typewriter down and went to the back of the plane and was sick on the floor, and that meant that, for the moment, now even he could not do any writing.

It took us four hours to get back to Paris by plane, and it had taken us eight months when we were going the other way. We sat in the plane trying to look out of the small windows at the country below, trying to recognize something when we flew over beaten towns, realizing now how rapidly we were putting it all behind us, all of the ground that had been taken so slowly and at that great cost.

"Do you remember," I said to Gordon Fraser, "when we said we would go back the way we came?"

Fraser worked for the Blue Network, and we called him "The Little Colonel." I think he could have taken over a regiment, he knew so much about it, and one day during the Bulge when I went up to a company we had all been with some days before, the captain asked me about him.

"How's that little radio fella who was here with you that time?" he said.

"Gordon Fraser?" I said. "He's fine."

"The day after you two were here," the captain said, "he came up alone, and he made the attack with us. The kid carrying the ammo for the machine gun got hit, so your friend picked up the ammo cases and carried them up to the gun. He's a hell of a guy."

If I hadn't known it before, I knew it then, because Fraser had never mentioned it. Years later, when I used to drop in to see him at NBC in New York, where he was working on "Monitor," I knew the rest of them in that office didn't know what he was or what he had done in the war.

"What we said we were going to do," I said to him, as we looked down out of that plane flying back, "was follow every side road and stop and walk in particular fields and examine hillsides we remember. We'd go into houses and cellars we slept in, and go over all of it again so we might understand it better and never forget it."

"I know," Fraser said, "but now let's just get home."

There were ten of us in the room on the ship in officer country, but down in the holds they were stacked in bunks four tiers high. There were 7,000 on what, when the Italians had her and called her the *Conte Grande*, had carried 1,000 passengers in luxury. Among the 7,000 there were 3,000 of what the Army called RAMPS, for Recovered American Military Personnel. They had been shot down over Berlin or captured at Kasserine or in the Ardennes, and they had survived the prison camps at Sagan and Barth and Hammelburg, and they had bad stomachs. They were supposed to be careful about what they ate, but they stood in the chow lines for hours like everyone else, and they ate everything and were sick.

In that room we were just as we had been back in Weimar. We read and slept and played cards for eleven days. We didn't talk about any of it any more, until the last night out when somebody broke out a bottle we didn't know he had been saving and put it on the table— and we heard some truth.

There was one I had traveled with a lot in the jeep because we wanted to see the same things and because he laughed a lot and relaxed me. If we were behind a wall and had to make a run for it, or if we had to go down a stretch of road, he always said the thing that got us out from behind the wall or down the road.

He was a very good mimic, and at night he was our best entertainment. He turned the things that had happened to us during the day into comedy bits, and we spent much time laughing with him. We knew he had been in the Pacific before he joined us in Europe, and now he was sitting with us around the bottle and his voice was rising and cracking.

"For Tarawa we drew lots," he said, "and I got it. I got it, but then I was afraid to go and they got slaughtered, and because I was afraid to go they sent me home."

We did not know what to say. I had had no idea of what he had been carrying, behind those walls and facing those roads, when he got me out. I tried to say something and somebody else said something but it didn't do any good, and so we just let him try to cry it out in our room on the ship coming home.

The next morning when we came through the Narrows, there was a fog over the Lower Bay, and they were lined four deep along the rails. On the starboard side in the last row there were three kids with First Armored patches on their shoulders, and they were looking over toward where you could just make out the parachute jump at Coney Island, and they said they were trying to see the Statue of Liberty. They said they had been captured at Faid Pass in Africa in February of 1943, and that one of the German guards at Fuerstenberg had told them they would never see the Statue of Liberty again, and I told him that the statue would show up off the other side.

"Look, sir," the Marine guard who was standing there said. "I know they want to see the Statue of Liberty. There are seven thousand guys on this ship who want to see the Statue of Liberty, and if I let them all go on that side, this damn thing will tip over."

"But these guys have been prisoners for more than two years," I said.

"We got three thousand of them that were prisoners," the Marine guard said. "What am I supposed to do?"

"Look the other way," I said.

I led them over to the port side, the big ship listing that way now, and all along the rows at the rail you could hear, "Where? Where?" I could just make it out, just a shadow in the fog, and I tried to point it out to the three kids.

"I think I can see it," the one from Illinois said to the other two. "If you'd ever seen it before, I think you could make it out. You see that something a little dark and kind of sticking up in the gray?"

"Yea, I think I can see it," the one from North Dakota said. "I'm sure I can."

"I'm sure I can, too," the one from Kentucky said. "That's got to be it there."

"That Kraut has got to be dead now," the one from Illinois said.

"Yeah, and we made a liar out of him, too," the one from North Dakota said.

It was eleven days on the end of a long time, and when I reached out to push the bell in the apartment entrance, my finger shook so that I had to breathe deeply and steady it. When the buzzer sounded I kicked the door open and I held it with my body and moved my old black bag and my barracks bag and my typewriter into the lobby.

I stood at the foot of the stairs and I was shaking. I swung the barracks bag onto my back and took the typewriter in one hand and I left the old black bag and I climbed the three flights of stairs. I climbed the stairs as hard as I could to keep from crying, and my wife stood in the doorway. She looked small and frail, and I could not begin to tell her, no less write it. There was so much that had finally ended.

D-Day Relived

from *Collier's*, 1954

It was about ten o'clock in the morning when we reached the crossroad just west of Formigny. The mist was still blowing inland off the Channel, coming across the green field to the right and, where there were trees, coming between the trees.

Ten years had passed since the Americans had been here, but he remembered the crossroad very well—the cavalry on the one corner and the battle monuments on the three others—and he turned the small gray Peugeot to the right and drove down the narrow winding black-top, hemmed in between the thick bulk of the hedgerows, until it widened out, where the new road curves through the center of Vierville-sur-Mer.

"The Vierville church," he said now, measuring the words and standing there and looking up at it. "A lot of Americans who landed on the beach will remember the Vierville church."

Next to the church is the walled graveyard, built up above the surface of the road. The church itself is gutted still, the roof gone and only a few fragments of stained glass still sticking in the windows, but from the front a new steeple points up into the sky.

"The Vierville church," he said again. "Bud, that was one of the old landmarks we studied a lot in England before the invasion. We studied it over and over."

The boy said nothing. He is fourteen years old now, named after his father, and has brown, slightly wavy hair and blue eyes. He was wearing crepe-soled shoes and blue jeans, a blue plaid shirt and a red corduroy jacket, and all of his memories of the war are involved with the small white house with the big mulberry tree in the back yard on South Bridge Street in Brady, Texas.

There was a hut in the tree, and the small boy would play there and, in the mornings, he would stand in the front yard and watch the trucks filled with German prisoners heading out to the farms. In the late afternoons he would see them come back, and he remembers the machine guns on the trucks and the Germans neither laughing nor shouting but just standing in the trucks as they went by. Now the boy looked up at the steeple.

"You haven't any idea how that old church used to worry us," his father said.

"Why?" the boy said.

"Because of the observation it gave the Germans," his father said. "The Channel is only about a half mile down the road here, and the Germans used all these church steeples for observation. That's why we had to shoot the steeple down."

In 1932, James Earl Rudder had received his academic degree and his commission as a second lieutenant, Infantry Reserve, from Texas A&M. He had played center for Matty Bell, but that first summer, at the depth of the depression, he dug ditches. From 1933 to 1938 he coached football and taught at Brady High School. He was coaching at John Tarleton College, in Stephenville, Texas, when he went on active duty in 1941 at Fort Sam Houston.

"It's a funny thing," Rudder said. "We shoot down the steeple, and that's the first thing the French build back, even before they build the church."

He drove through the small intersection of the town. Two houses away from one corner two workmen were just starting to put back the stones that had lain in a pile for ten years, and as the car went by they stopped, turning to watch it. Then Rudder drove down a slight slope that bent around to the left between hedgerows, and as the car came out of the curve, still on the slope, you could see a large new yellow fieldstone house, still not completed, and, straight ahead, the gray-blue waters and the mist above them.

"There's your English Channel, Bud," he said.

"There?" the boy said.

"That's right, and that's where we came in, the men who didn't hit the cliff. A lot of American soldiers came up this road we're on now, because it was the main exit road for everybody who came in on this end of the beach."

The car was stopped in the middle of the sloping road, and the man and the boy just sat there looking down across the top of the two German concrete emplacements and at the tilted hulk of a hollow concrete floating pier that had been driven by a storm onto the shore. Then Rudder released the brake and the car rolled down the road toward the emplacements and then stopped on a wide, sweeping curve.

"And there's Omaha Beach."

He had known it was there, he said later, but still it came as a surprise. There it was, three and a half miles of deserted crescent, curving eastward, the blue-gray waters of the Channel on the left, the white waves rolling up onto the stretch of smooth, tan sand.

"What's this gun here?" the boy said.

The car was parked now on the rise behind the two concrete emplacements. The boy had run around to the front of the first of them, and was looking at the long, rusting barrel that pointed down the beach.

"That's an old 88," Rudder said. "You can see how it was set here to cover the beach."

"I wish we could go in this blockhouse," the boy said, "but there's this screen over the front of it."

"You can see they had direct hits from the Navy on it," his father said, "but they never could get that gun. That's why the soldiers had to come in and take it."

The boy had run now to the second emplacement, and his father walked after him. The father was wearing black shoes, gray sharkskin trousers, a reddish plaid shirt, a mixed-tan sport jacket, a covert-cloth topcoat, and a light tan fedora.

"Can I go in this one?" the boy said. "You can get in, and there's a big machine gun here."

"That was covering the beach, too," the father said and then he swept his hand below, "and right over there is where Frank Corder got hit. They were trying to make it up here."

Frank Corder was a young captain from Rock Springs, Texas, who had joined the Rangers late. Rudder had handpicked the 2nd Ranger Battalion at Camp Forrest, Tennessee, in July of 1943. The battalion had shipped to England in December of that year, and it was a month later, when he was in Northern Ireland recruiting volunteers to be used as a reserve after the invasion, that he signed up Corder, whom he had met before. After the war he and Corder went into the general-appliance and

tire business in Brady. Now Corder has three children
and is a livestock dealer.

"He lost his left eye and some of his teeth on this
beach," Rudder said. "He still gets some pain, on and
off, but I'll never forget one day I was trying to take him
on a livestock deal, the way you will, and he squinted at
me and he said, 'Colonel, remember this. I've still got
one good eye.'"

Where the sand ends at the top of the beach the
white, smooth, egg-shaped stones begin. There used
to be about fifty feet of them, but now the French have
built a six-foot sloping concrete and fieldstone seawall
that covers most of them. On top of the seawall there
is a curbed sidewalk and a two-lane roadway that runs
the length of the beach, for the convenience of sight-
seers.

"What's this?" the boy said. "A gas mask?"

They had walked along the sidewalk and then down
one of the flights of stairs leading to the beach. They had
crossed the stones and Rudder was just standing, looking
east along the sand, when the boy ran up to him with the
olive-drab rubber face piece in his hand.

"An old American gas mask," Rudder said turning it
over in his hands. "The old canister gas mask. I didn't
think you'd find anything here."

He turned now, and started to walk slowly back toward the two concrete gun emplacements. Then he
stopped, and with the toe of his right shoe he started to
scuff into the smooth, tight sand.

"Can you imagine," he said, "some poor American kid
trying to find cover in this?"

"It sure is pretty now, with the waves and everything,"
the boy said. "You'd never think there was any fighting
here."

The late morning sun had finally started to eat through the haze, and you could begin to feel its warmth. It was quiet on the deserted beach, with just the soft rhythmic slur of the waves and the occasional cry of a wheeling gull.

"I want you to try to picture this, Bud," Rudder said, turning again to look along the length of the beach and sweeping it with his right arm. "A lot of American boys died here."

"Yes, sir," the boy said.

"You've got to picture this whole beach covered with all kinds of equipment, with boats and trucks and jeeps and tanks, a lot of them wrecked, and with American soldiers, and the Germans firing into them from the high ground and a smoke haze over everything."

"Yes, sir."

"You remember General Cota, Bud?"

"Yes, sir."

Major General Norman D. Cota, of Philadelphia, was assistant commander of the 29th Infantry Division and took the 116th Regiment into Omaha on the right flank of the 1st Infantry Division. Later he became commander of the 28th Infantry Division, and Rudder led the 109th Regiment, under Cota, through the Bulge and on to Germany.

"Here's where he did his good work, getting the boys up off the beach," Rudder said. "A lot of them just froze from the horror of it, and he got them up."

"Is he the one gave me that toy watch?" the boy said.

"His wife gave it to you."

"I remember."

They walked along the beach together, not saying anything, the boy swinging the mask at his side and watching the white waves slush up onto the sand. Then the father turned back toward the smooth white stones at the foot of the seawall and the boy followed him. When Rudder reached the stones he kneeled down. With one hand he began to pore among them, to the smaller stones underneath.

"Here," he said, handing three or four to the boy. "Put these in your pocket."

The boy, kneeling beside his father, took the stones and looked at them. Then he looked at his father. "Why?" he said.

"Take them back to Buddy and Elene and Mary Glenn," he said, speaking of Corder's children. "These stones are off the beach where their daddy was hit. They might want them."

We left the beach and drove back through Vierville and then turned right and followed the blacktop coastal road west toward Grandcamp-les-Bains. Looking down from the crest of the road we recognized the town at once, the red-tiled roofs that many an American Navy man will remember when he thinks of the little fishing and bathing community of a couple of hundred houses that stood, by a miracle of war, almost untouched between Omaha Beach and Utah Beach.

We drove through the narrow, cobblestoned street, to the rectangular quay west of the town. In the basin below the quay the black-bodied fishing boats, side by side, were rising slowly with the tide, and on some of them nets were drying, strung from their masts and booms. On the quay a half-dozen fishermen were standing, and they turned and looked at us when we drove up and stopped the car.

"But it is not necessary to go by boat," one of them said, when I told them what we wanted to do.

"I know," I said.

"It is very easy to go with your car," he said, standing there on the quay in the sunlight and pointing. "You drive here through the village and five kilometers on the left you will see the road."

"But you do not understand," I said. "The day of the invasion, this gentleman here, was a colonel of the American Rangers. He was the first American to land at Pointe du Hoe."

An American Army cartographer made the error in reading the French maps—he mistook the "c" for an "e," and so in the American military annals it is "Pointe du Hoe," while to the French it is, of course, Pointe du Hoc.

"He landed at Pointe du Hoc?"

"Yes."

"He mounted the cliff?"

"Yes."

They looked at one another and then at Rudder. It was easy to read their minds. Rudder is forty-four years old now. His brown hair is graying at the temples. He has added four inches around the waist and about thirty pounds, and he was standing now, his topcoat open, try-ing to understand some of this.

"It was very difficult and very dangerous," one of them said, "what he did."

That is how we got the boat, an old, dirty-green, twenty-foot launch with an engine in the middle only partly housed, and the oily water slopping in the pit. There were three Frenchmen in it—the old man with a week's growth of gray beard who owns it and the two younger ones—and they sat in silence together near the tiller and when, now and then, we looked back at them they would smile and nod their heads.

The sun was bright now, so the Channel was very blue around us, and when we had passed beyond the break-water the old man turned east. Now we could see it un-fold, the sharp nose sticking way out into the Channel and beyond the nose, the dark cliffs rising seventy-five to one hundred feet straight up from the narrow beach.

"There it is," Rudder said quietly, leaning with his elbows on the waist-high forward deck, with his son beside him. "Pointe du Hoe."

He had heard of "Pointe du Hoe" for the first time five months before the invasion, in a second-floor room in London behind a whitestone front, with the blackout drapes drawn and four of them standing there with the maps and photos on the table. Rudder and Max Schneider, a colonel out of Iowa who had trained the 1st Ranger Battalion, had come up by train from Bude, in Cornwall, and they got their D-Day assignment from Truman Thorson, the tall, thin-cheeked colonel out of Birmingham, Alabama, who was G-3 for First Army, and from the officer who was Thorson's assistant.

"When we got a look at it," Rudder said, "Max just whistled once through his teeth. He had a way of doing that. He'd made three landings already, but I was just a country boy coaching football a year and a half before. It would almost knock you out of your boots."

The cliffs rise as high as a nine-story office building, and on the tableland above them the Germans had observation on the whole Channel area and had mounted and were casemating guns capable of firing onto both Omaha and Utah beaches. It was the Germans' strongest point and it had to be taken. It was what General Omar N. Bradley was later to describe as the most difficult assignment he had ever given a soldier in his military career.

Rudder and Schneider took the assignment back to Bude, put a twenty-four-hour guard on the door, and at night would get out the maps and the pictures and study them. Every time the Germans dug another trench or set another mine field the P-38 reconnaissance planes, skimming over the cliffs, got pictures of it. The French brought back samples of the soil and of the cliffs, and Rudder, in England, held the dirt in his hands and finally made the decision to scale the cliffs.

"Do you think," the boy said now, "we'll be able to climb it?"

The two of them, the father and the son, were leaning forward and studying the shaded face of the cliff. The old Frenchman was still taking the boat parallel to it about a quarter mile out, waiting for us to tell him to turn it in.

"No, son," Rudder said. "We won't."

"But you climbed it before."

"I was younger then, son, and we trained for it. We had the special equipment, too."

In the months before the invasion they had found, at Swanage, on the south coast of England, cliffs of almost exactly the same height and composition, and they climbed these, sometimes three times a day. They had ropes, affixed to steel grapnels to be propelled to the cliff top by rockets, and they also carried four-foot sections of tubular steel ladders and had mounted, on four DUKWs, one-hundred-foot extension ladders borrowed from the London Fire Department.

"It wasn't," the boy said, "a nice day like this, was it?"

"It was a good deal colder and rougher," his father said, "and early in the morning."

It had been 4:05 in the morning and still dark when the Rangers loaded into the British LCAs from the Amsterdam and the Ben Machree. They were ten miles from shore and there were 225 of them and they had to start bailing with their helmets almost immediately. Twenty-one men from D Company had to be rescued by launch. One supply craft sank with only one survivor, and another threw its packs overboard to stay afloat.

"Can you imagine," Rudder said now, "anybody going up that thing?"

"It's twice as high as I thought," the boy said.

Lieutenant General Clarence R. Huebner, of New York, commanding the 1st Division and mounting the Omaha assault, had forbidden Rudder to lead the three companies of Rangers in. "We're not going to risk getting you knocked out in the first round," Huebner had said.

"I'm sorry to have to disobey you, sir," Rudder had replied, "but if I don't take it, it may not go."

Now the two younger Frenchmen moved forward quickly between us and, as the boat scraped down, they were in the water. They had on black knee boots and together they pulled the launch another couple of feet up onto the stones. Then they motioned, laughing, and one took the boy on his shoulders and the other took the father, and that is the way Rudder went in the second time, his topcoat open, his hat knocked back on his head and the Frenchman staggering a little under the weight of the 230 pounds.

"This is what we hoped to land in," Rudder said, looking down at the stony beach where the Frenchman had deposited him, "but what we got was bomb holes and muck."

The heavy bombers and the mediums had plastered the cliff, and the near misses had torn the beach open. Most of the Rangers debarked up to their shoulders in mud and water. The DUKWs with the ladders foundered and were useless. Most of the rocket-propelled ropes were so heavy from the wetting that the grapnels failed to carry to the cliff top.

"Right here," Rudder said, "is where Trevor touched down next to me. He was a British commando colonel, Travis H. Trevor, who volunteered to give us a hand and he just stepped out, right here, when a bullet hit his helmet and drove him to his knees. I helped him up and the blood was starting to trickle down his forehead, but he was a great big, black-haired son of a gun—one of those staunch Britishers—and he just looked up at the top of the cliff and he said, 'The dirty ——.'"

Fifteen men were lost on the narrow strip of stones. Some of the wounded crawled from the waterline to the base of the cliff.

"Hey, Daddy!" the boy called. "Come here."

Between two large boulders against the base of the cliff the boy had found a hollow shaft of rusted metal protruding from among the smaller stones. He had started to scoop the stones away with his hands, and now one of the Frenchmen got down on his knees and we watched him dig until, smiling, he got up and handed it to us.

"A grapnel," Rudder said, taking it. "One of the grapnels."

There was the hollow shaft, about six inches long and an inch and a half in diameter, and then, at the head of it, the six bent prongs, petal-like, the whole about the size and shape of a small boat anchor. As Rudder held it and turned it over, the rust flaked into his hands.

"This is amazing," he said shaking his head. "After ten years you can walk back here and find one of the grapnels on the ground."

"Can we take it home?" the boy said.

"Certainly we'll take it home," Rudder said. "This must be the last of those grapnels."

He handed it to the Frenchman and pointed to the boat. The Frenchman nodded and ran to the boat and put it in, and now the boy was gone again and the father stood looking up at the top of the cliff, and the jagged dark line against the sky.

"Will you tell me how we did this?" he said. "Anybody would be a fool to try this. It was crazy then, and it's crazy now."

When the naval fire had lifted from the cliff top the Germans had come out of their holes and trenches and concrete emplacements and, in addition to using small arms, they had dropped grenades on the heads of the Americans. In less than five minutes, however, the first Ranger had scaled the cliff, and within thirty minutes the whole force, minus casualties, climbing the ropes attached to the grapnels that had been rocket-launched, had reached the top.

"*M'sieur!*" It was one of the two younger Frenchmen, who had walked ahead of us, west along the small beach. He was standing now, calling and waving to us, close to where the nose of the point knifes into the Channel. "*Regardez, M'sieur!*"

"A rope," Rudder said. "There's still a rope here."

It was a whole length of three-quarter-inch single rope. It had taken on the mustard color of the clay that had washed down around it, and it hung there on the serpentine curve of the slope, still fastened to the iron pickets driven every ten feet into the cliff, its end flapping loose about six feet from the ground.

"Lapres' boat put it there," Rudder said.

Lieutenant Theodore E. Lapres, Jr., was from Philadelphia, and, about three weeks later, he lost a foot outside of Beaumont, just west of Cherbourg. Twice the rope had been cut that first day, and two men were hit getting it up there.

"*M'sieur?*" the Frenchman said. He was pulling at the loose end and waving it as if to detach it, laughing at Rudder.

"No," Rudder said, shaking his head.

"Can we climb it, Daddy?" asked the boy, who had run up to us now.

"No," Rudder said, shaking his head.

"Why?"

"Because," Rudder said, "we're not going to get you hurt, son, on this cliff . . . "

On the way back to Grandcamp the sea was running with us, so it took us less than a half hour. Once, Rudder noticed the rusted grapnel lying on the floor of the launch and he picked it up and looked at it closely again and shook his head. Then he put it carefully back on the floor of the boat.

"*Grappin!*" the same young Frenchman said, nodding, and then he laughed and, with his hands and by shaking his body, he made the motions of climbing a rope. "A good souvenir."

When we got back to the quay there was a small group waiting for us, a half-dozen fishermen and a thin, dark-haired, middle-aged man from the Information Bureau of the town. With him was a younger man, in his mid-thirties, and they wanted to know if they could show us the ground where the fighting had taken place at the top of the cliff.

"They can show us if they want to," Rudder said, smiling, "but I know it better than I know the palm of my hand."

The Rangers, fighting until relief could come up from Omaha, had been isolated on the cliff top for two days and two nights. About a half mile of flat, pastured table-land had spread back from the V edge of the cliff to the road that runs east and west between Vierville and Grandcamp, but when the Rangers had reached the top they found it an erupted wasteland of dirt and mud, made unrecognizable by the heavy preparatory bombing from the air and the heavy shelling from the sea.

"Now you stay close to us, Bud," Rudder said. "Don't go running off."

"I just want to see," the boy said.

Rudder had parked the Peugeot on a small patch of level grass at the end of the hedgerowed lane that runs from the blacktop out toward the point of the cliff. We had started along a path between the shoulder-high growth of dark-green thorn bushes with the stalks of small, tight yellow flowers that the French call *ajonc* and the British call gorse.

"There wasn't this growth here then," Rudder said. "It was all just ripped-open dirt."

The bomb and shell holes, one opening into another and some of them thirty feet across and ten feet deep, were grown with grass now, and Rudder picked a path between them. Then he came upon the concrete block-house, standing dome-roofed about eight feet above the ground, open toward the Channel, and its floor strewn with concrete rubble. He looked at it a moment, then called the boy.

"Bud," he said, "come back here. I want you to see this."

He walked down the two steps among the pieces of broken concrete, and the boy followed him. Then Rudder turned around.

"This is where the shell hit," he said, pointing up just above his head to a broken section of the corner where two rusted reinforcing rods protruded. "They say it wasn't from one of our ships, but when you look at the direction, it had to be.

"The artillery captain," he said, "a nice-looking, black-haired boy—I wish I could remember his name—was killed right here. The Navy lieutenant, who was spotting with us, fell right here." He pointed. "It knocked me over right here."

He pulled back the right sleeve of his topcoat, unbuttoned his shirt cuff, and exposed his forearm and the small red welt on it.

"Right under that," Rudder said, "is a piece of the concrete from right here."

"The colonel was wounded here?" the older of the two Frenchmen said.

"You carry it around in you for ten years," Rudder said, "and you bring it right back where it came from."

"I thought you had two pieces in there," the boy said, looking at his father's arm.

"I've thought about this a lot," Rudder said. "I mean, you wonder how close it really was, if it was as close as it seemed and how a man could live. The way I pictured it, you could just about reach up and touch the place where the shell hit, and you just about can."

The boy had found an old red-handled American toothbrush in the dust and broken concrete on the floor. He handed it to his father and his father looked at it and tossed it on the ground.

"Come around here with me," he said to the boy.

They walked around to the east of the blockhouse. The shelling had ripped half the concrete off the side, exposing horizontal rows of reinforcing rods. Rudder climbed up onto the second one and the boy climbed up beside him, where they could both look toward the lane.

"Earlier that morning we were right here," the father said. "The Navy lieutenant was on my right, where you are, the artillery captain was on my left and we were try-ing to direct fire over there when I got shot in the leg."

"Where was the German?" the boy said, turning.

"I don't know," Rudder said.

The first time the boy had ever seen the bullet wound had been in the little house on South Bridge Street, sit-ting one night in the parlor. His grandmother was there and his uncle and his aunt and his sister and his two cousins. Someone had asked about the wound and his fa-ther had rolled up the left pant leg and there, just above the knee, was the pink scar where the bullet had gone in and, on the other side, the pink scar where it had come out. It had been a clean penetration, and so it had not looked like much of a wound to the boy.

"This way, Bud," Rudder said now, calling again to the boy.

The boy had run ahead, running along the ridges between the bomb craters. There would be times when he would disappear completely in the growth, and then you would see his red corduroy jacket.

"I just want to see the CP," the boy said, coming back out of breath.

"You'll see it," Rudder said. "Just be patient."

"I think it's over there," the boy said, pointing over the rough ground and the green growth.

"You stick with me, son," Rudder said, "and you won't have to worry about where things are."

"But I can find it," the boy said.

"I'll find it," Rudder said. "I've been here before."

He walked as directly to it as you could, considering the turbulence of the ground. It had been his first command post in France, a hollow scooped out of the edge of the cliff by a bomb, and it was from here that he had sent out his first message: "Praise the Lord," the code meaning: "Rangers up cliff."

"Need ammunition and reinforcements," he had sent out later. "Many casualties."

"No reinforcements available," was the answer that had come back.

Now he stood in the middle of it, and the boy was at the edge, peering down where his father had once rope-climbed, down the sheer drop of about ninety feet, with the narrow stony beach below.

"Bud!"

"Yes?"

"Look, son. I want you to keep away from that edge."

"I'm just looking."

"You could fall off there, and I'd have to go home and face your mother."

"Is that where our flag was?" the boy said.

"No," Rudder said, pointing. "It was right over here."

They had anchored the American flag to the cliff with rocks. When the relief had come on D plus two the tankers had presumed that the Rangers had been annihilated, and so they had started to fire onto the point. He had waved the flag on a stick and the firing had stopped, and now the flag is in the wooden box in the den of the white limestone house in Brady. Along with the flag are the two German revolvers, the two German chrome-plated 2-mm shells, the two German knives, the French beret and the D.S.C., the Silver Star, the Bronze Star with cluster, the Purple Heart with cluster, the Croix de Guerre, and the Légion d'Honneur.

"Mommy finally got a box with a glass in front and put the medals in it and hung it on the wall," the boy had said one night. "Then it fell off the wall and broke to pieces, and after Mommy went to all that trouble Daddy just laughed."

Rudder climbed up now on one side of the scooped earth. He walked around to the side of the buried block-house.

"We got our first German prisoner right here," he said. "He was a little freckle-faced kid who looked like an American, and we were so proud of him, because when you're trying to get your first prisoner, it's like diving for pearls.

"Then I had a feeling there were more of them, and I told the Rangers to lead this kid ahead of them. They just started him around this corner when the Germans opened up out of the entrance and he fell dead, right here, face down with his hands still clasped on the top of his head."

"How many were in there?" the boy said.

"We killed one and got seven or eight out," Rudder said. "It was right here, too, that we left the artillery captain, lying right here on a litter when we took off on D plus two."

"We can go down in here," the boy said, calling up from down inside the entrance. "It's open and we might find something in here."

"He was only about twenty-five years old," Rudder said. "I'm sorry I've forgotten his name."

We walked back to the car and drove out the lane that leads off the point and then down another lane where Leonard G. Lomell, of Toms River, New Jersey, then a sergeant and later commissioned in the field, and Staff Sergeant Jack E. Kuhn, of Altoona, Pennsylvania, had found the big guns, hidden behind a hedgerow and set up to fire onto Utah Beach. The Americans had bashed in the sights and had blown the recoil mechanisms and the barrels with thermite grenades.

Now you could still see the gun pits dug into the drainage ditch along the hedgerow, almost covered with creeping vines. We walked down the green lane and then walked left along another hedgerow and then down across a hundred yards of field that, in season, would be a field of wheat.

"I want you to picture this, son," Rudder said.

The field was covered with a lush green, ankle-high growth of winter rye and clover. At the foot of the field was a mortared stone wall, about eighteen inches thick and four feet high.

"This is where Sergeant Petty had his squad, Bud," Rudder said, stopping where a rough opening still gaped in the top of the wall. "From here they could look right down into this valley."

"Was there any fighting here?" the boy said.

"There was a lot of fighting here, son," Rudder said. "That first night the Germans attacked right through that orchard there, and got around behind Petty, who was way out here."

Sergeant William Petty had come from Cohutta, Georgia. He was a pale-faced, unimposing kid with slick blond hair and no upper teeth, and he kept coming to Rudder during the heat of that summer of '43 in Tennessee. Rudder had turned him down twice and then, when he had gone over to screen the 80th Division volunteers, Petty was in the front line.

"I thought I discouraged you, Petty," Rudder had said.

"Please sir," Petty had said. "I'll look better when I get my teeth."

"All right," Rudder had said. "If you want the Rangers that bad, I'll take you."

Petty was made a Browning automatic rifleman. When he got up to platoon sergeant he asked Rudder if he could still carry the heavy BAR. He carried it up the cliff and killed, they figured afterward, about thirty Germans with it, and there are many among the Rangers who today still say that Petty saved their lives.

"These were brave men, here," Rudder said now to the boy.

The boy had thrown his leg over the wall and was looking at the hole that Petty and his men had knocked into the top of the wall to give them a better field of fire for the BAR. He nodded his head.

"You have to remember, son, that it was pitch dark and they didn't know how many Germans there were or where they were."

"Yes, sir."

"You remember how you used to feel when you had to go to the henhouse at night at the ranch?"

"Yes, sir."

Rudder turned around and looked back up the slope of the green field. With the toe of his right shoe he made a pass at the rye and clover.

"If I had this kind of cover at home," he said, "I'd sure put some sheep on it."

He finished with his piece of ground. It was late afternoon and we drove back, through that crossroad outside Formigny and east to Bayeux. That night we sat in the small linoleumed lobby of the Lion d'Or waiting for the BBC news on the small radio standing on the radiator cover. The boy had gone up to bed.

"You wonder so long," Rudder said, "what it would be like to come back. Then you come back and it's hard to know what you feel."

We were alone in the lobby except for the woman in the black dress leaning on the desk with her elbows and watching us and then turning her eyes down when we happened to look at her.

"It was hard to believe when it was going on," Rudder said. "It's even harder to believe now."

When Rudder had come back from the war he had lost himself in his family and his work. There were the two children before he went to war—the boy and Margaret Ann, who is now twelve—and three after the war—Linda, who is seven, Jane, five, and Robert, born last April. There is the office at the Brady Aviation Plant of the Intercontinental Manufacturing Company, Inc., where he is vice president. He is on the State Democratic Committee and the State Board of Welfare, and for six years was mayor of Brady.

"You think of the wonderful kids you had with you," he said. "You think that if you could have men like that

around you in a peacetime world, men as devoted as
that, there wouldn't be anything you couldn't accomplish."

"What about Bud?" I said, after a while. "What do you
suppose he thinks of all this?"

"It's hard to say," Rudder said. "I kinda hope he'll
think a lot about it in years to come."

I thought of the younger of the two Frenchmen from
Grandcamp, watching the boy on the top of the point.
The Frenchman had been unable to understand what
the boy or his father was saying, but he was able to com-
prehend it, nevertheless.

"The father, he tries to explain to the boy," the
Frenchman had said, "but the boy, he looks for sou-
venirs."

"Yes," I had said. "He was four years old at the time of
the war."

"It is like it was with me," the Frenchman had said.
"When I was young my father would tell me about his
war, the war of '14. I could not understand. Then came
the war of '40 and '44. After that I understood war. I understood my war, and I understood the war of my father."

The next morning we had breakfast in the new hotel
in Carentan, where, right next to the bar, there is a
frosted wall light with the Screaming Eagle patch of the
101st Airborne painted on it. We had lunch in Saint-Lô,
that was dust ten years ago and against which, ten years
ago, we measured all destruction from then on.

That afternoon we drove south and then, finally, east
toward Paris through the winding, climbing country of
the Falaise gap, where the Americans and the British had
slaughtered most of what was left of the German Army
that had tried to hold Normandy. It was about midafternoon, and we had just passed through Argentan, when
the boy spoke up from the backseat.

"What did we do with the grapnel, Daddy?" he asked.

"I'm afraid," his father said, "that we forgot it. We left it in the boat."

"But we were going to take it home," the boy said, "for a souvenir."

"I'm sorry, son," his father said, "but we just forgot it."

I thought about the grapnel, lying in the bottom of the boat. We had paid the old man well for his boat and so, I supposed, he would leave it there for a while, thinking that we might still come back, Then one day, I imagined, he would be hurrying forward to check his lines or to catch the engine before it coughed out, and his foot or his pant leg would become entangled in the grapnel. Then he would stop and pick it up and look at it and think of us. Finally he would shrug his shoulders and then, taking a last look at it, he would drop it overboard. The sun would be shining, as I imagined it, and the grapnel would sink through the blue waters to the bottom of the English Channel.

It was the last of the grapnels and it had taken ten years for it to find its place, so that would be the end of it all.

As it turned out, that was not quite the end of it all. Even as I had found Earl Rudder in General Omar Bradley's autobiography, Texas found him in the cover story in Collier's. *The following year, Allan Shivers, campaigning for his second term as governor, asked James Earl Rudder to introduce him at political rallies around the state, and the next year, when the Texas Land Office was hit by scandal, he appointed him interim land commissioner. In 1957, Rudder was elected to the office, and two years later, he was made president of Texas A&M and, in 1965, of the entire Texas A&M system. When he retired from the Army Reserve in 1967, he was a major general, and had made, at the Army's invitation, two more visits back to "Pointe du Hoe."*

The top of the cliff has changed. In 1954, Robert Ravelet, head of the Local Information Bureau, had told us that he had been attempting for years to persuade the proper authorities in Paris to appropriate the land as a memorial to the Americans who had captured it. In 1960, at an obelisk of native stone erected at the cliff edge, the thirty-one acres were dedicated, and in 1978, the preserve was turned over to the American Battle Monuments Commission. The access road has been named Allée du Colonel Rudder, *and now, each year, thousands of tourists, Germans among them, visit the site.*

w.c.h., 1982

On March 23, 1970, Major General Earl Rudder died at the age of fifty-nine in St. Luke's Hospital, in Houston, of circulatory collapse. In 1973, the $10 million J. Earl Rudder Conference Center, an auditorium complex surmounted by an eleven-story tower, was dedicated on the Texas A&M campus. In 1998, in Austin, the James Earl Rudder State Office Building was dedicated, and in 1990 at A&M Margaret Rudder Hall, the four-floor women's dormitory, named for his widow, was opened to one hundred and fifty residents. In 1994 a life-size bronze statue of Rudder was unveiled on a grassy knoll overlooking the University Center.

Each year, on the anniversary of his death, a memorial service is held by the French in Crique, near Grandcamp. His elder son, James Earl Rudder, Jr., whom I knew as the fourteen-year-old Bud, is now sixty-two years of age and retired from automotive sales and living in Dallas.

w.c.h., 2002

The Day We Met
the Russians

from *50 Plus,* 1985

"Head for Eagle Gulch!" one of the American photographers was yelling as the two mobs swarmed toward each other. "We'll cut 'em off at the pass!"

Those words won't resound through American annals with the words of John Paul Jones about just beginning to fight, of David Glasgow Farragut about torpedoes and full speed ahead or of William Prescott about the whites of enemy eyes. They belong, however, on the monument that stands today at Torgau, in East Germany, as epitomizing the daffiness that history will undoubtedly underplay, if it doesn't ignore, in its record of World War II and that day 40 years ago when the American and Russian armies finally met in the heart of Germany.

History is written by participants, by what they do and say, then rewritten and edited by historians. Whenever, as now, American and Russian diplomats sit down at another table, trying once more to find some common ground other than fear, and someone says that if we could only leave it to the people all would be well, I remember that day—a day that history should chronicle as being as saddening as it was absurd.

At about 12:30 P.M. on April 25, 1945, a patrol of a half dozen American GI's, wandering around where they shouldn't have been in the no-man's-land between the American and Russian armies in central Germany, reached the Elbe River at Strehla. On the opposite bank they saw a group of what regrettably came to be called "G. Ivans" waving the Russian flag. Within minutes the two groups had hooked up. Four hours later, in Torgau, about 16 miles to the north of Strehla, four other Americans, similarly exceeding orders, fell in with another contingent of Comrades; and the next day the rest of us got in on it and turned world history into low comedy.

For those of us who had been covering the war in Northern Europe since D-Day, the world-awaited linking up of the American and Russian forces, guaranteeing the end of Adolf Hitler's Third Reich, appeared to be the penultimate story. If the two conquering and converging armies, still battling German remnants between them, could just keep from firing into each other's ranks, the German surrender could only follow.

The plan, arrived at by the two powers, called for the American 1st and 9th armies to stop at the Mulde River and for the Russian 1st Ukranian Army to halt at the Elbe, some 18 miles to the east. Tentative patrols would be sent out, like antennae sensing and seeing but not quite touching, until the stage directors on both sides could set the scene for a ceremony befitting the occasion.

For days dozens of us, newspapermen, radio reporters, photographers and newsreel cameramen, had been touring the central German state of Thuringia, racing up and down the front, skirting pockets of recalcitrant Nazis, dodging military traffic and swarms of refugees while chasing rumors that the Russians were nearby. A jeepload of correspondents heading in one direction would pass a similar jeepload heading in the other. Fifty yards down the road each jeep would slide to a halt, its occupants fearful that the others knew something they did not, and shortly they would be passing each other again, heading back toward where they had come from.

Meanwhile, the more experienced of us, assuming that the honor of fronting for America would fall to the most deserving unit currently on line, started making book on the logical candidates. The two favorites were infantry divisions that had been fighting in Africa and Sicily before Normandy, although there was some support for the airborne as well as the armored divisions that had been spearheading the drive east since Paris. I mention them not by number, for the best led had no corner on courage; and it is no disparagement of the bravery of the individual soldier nor does it dishonor the dead to report that no one bet on the 69th Infantry.

On April 22, three days before the 69th stumbled onto the Russians and 30 miles to the west of the Elbe, the 69th had captured Leipzig at an inexplicable and inexcusable cost in American lives. With the collapse of German resistance obviously imminent, they had sent a column of 13 tanks and five tank destroyers down the main street leading to Leipzig's city hall, with an infantry of 185 men clinging to the sides. As the men moved down that thousand yards or so, the Germans on rooftops and in windows opened up with machine guns and bazookas, and when the blood-spattered armor reached its destination, of those 185 men only 68 had made it.

At least now it could be said for the 69th that it had proceeded with caution and spent no lives. In fact, more truth probably emerged than if the meeting had been left to the stagery of the big planners rather than to the natural instincts of the participants and the creative imagination of those geniuses of improvisation, the American photographic press on that early afternoon of April 26.

"Get a load of this Russki!" one of the press was calling to a colleague. "Let's get one of our guys with him!"

The Russian, on our side of the Elbe, had been firing his automatic rifle aimlessly across a stone wall and into the river when the photographers discovered him. Finding himself the center of attention he held up his hand, disappeared and returned with a leafed-out branch, behind which he was now posing as a sniper. The photographers decided to couple him with a GI and compound the fakery that in itself tells a truth of our time.

The Elbe at Torgau is about a hundred yards wide and swiftly moving. The Germans had blown the two local bridges, and the only water transport was aboard a half dozen slim, highly varnished two-man racing shells of the Torgau Rowing Club.

On our side of the river, amid the celebrating soldiers of the two forces, about 300 homeward-bound Russian civilians—old men, women and children, with baby carriages, pots and pans, valises and bedding—sat and stood on the bank awaiting their turns aboard the shells. Most of them were still there when, at 3 P.M., an hour before he was scheduled to meet his Russian counterpart, Major General Emil Reinhardt, commanding the 69th, strode down to the waterfront with his artillery general and his chief of staff beside him.

"Get that woman off the boat!" someone in the general's party was shouting. "Get her off there! The general needs that boat!"

Firmly planted in the bow of the only available shell was a Russian woman, about as broad as she was tall, her belongings crammed into a baby carriage athwart the prow in front of her. She was going home after only she knew how many years and how many indignities of slave labor, and no brass or sense of history was going to move her.

"Reinhardt's still lucky," someone said, watching the general and his staff cross squatting behind the woman. "Washington had to *stand*."

On the east bank, a half dozen Russians were still sawing and hammering on what was intended to be the ceremonial platform when the general's party, which had now attracted soldiers from both sides, as well as American correspondents, photographers and cameramen, started up from the river bank. At the platform the throng paused, confused, until someone spotted a swarm of Russians, centering around their own general, starting down from the red brick barracks at the top of the slope about 100 yards away, and the Eagle Gulch cry went up.

"To your horses, men!" someone else was shouting. "Charge!"

As the two hordes converged, the generals were not only face to face but belly to belly. There were shouts about giving them room, elbowing, shoving and cursing, until somehow the Russian commander—Major General Zagoveniev Rusakov, of the 58th Division—managed to turn around; and the two sides, now one host, started up the hill toward the barracks, the dust rising around it.

"What a rat race!" one of the American photographers was calling to another. "I haven't been in anything like this since I left the States."

"If everybody woulda just moved back," the other was calling back, "we coulda all got our shots!"

An hour later, back on the west bank of the river, the Americans were swapping lapel insignia, fountain pens, cigarette lighters, nail clippers and whatever else the

Russians would accept for the enameled Red Stars they wear on their caps. One of the Americans was proffering a new dollar bill to a Russian astride a motorcycle.

"He's giving a lecture," the interpreter was saying of the Russian, who was shaking his head. "It's about the hammer and sickle."

"Then try this guy," the American said, holding the bill out to another Russian, who had been watching and now began to frown.

"He also says no," the interpreter said. "He says Americans have all the money and they think money buys everything."

"But tell him it's just a souvenir," the American said. "It's the only souvenir I have. Tell him it's not meant . . . "

"Now he's giving a lecture on capitalism," the interpreter said. "You can see he's angry."

"Oh, the heck with this," one of the other Americans said. He took the dollar bill, stuck it in the hand of the Russian and, at the same time, reached up and pulled the Red Star off the Russian's cap. He handed the star to his companion and they both turned their backs and walked away.

On March 5, 1946, in Fulton, Mo., Winston Churchill would apprise the world that "an iron curtain has descended across the Continent." It had begun to fall the previous April 26, at Torgau, Germany, about 4 P.M.

The Retreat at Mons

from *True*, 1950

In the first World War, the British suffered their first defeat at Mons. They moved into the line on August 21, 1914. On August 23 the Germans attacked. The British fought well that day, but the French gave way at Charleroi. And on August 24 the British had to pull out, losing more men than they had lost holding the line. The Germans had them outnumbered and there were some British who wandered around lost for days. The German infantry swarmed in like gray-green locusts. It was a major retreat, although some history books have it as an orderly withdrawal.

We crossed the Belgian border and went for Mons at 4 o'clock in the afternoon on September 2, 1944. The sun was shining and it was good tank country and we were moving on a good blacktop road. When the first tank crossed the border it stopped. The general was riding behind it in his peep, which is what the armored guys called a jeep, and he got out and the first thing he did was urinate. That is the kind of a commander he was, and that is what he thought of World War II.

There was a building up the road on the left. We pulled up in front of it. There was a small restaurant and bar on the first floor and the Belgians who owned it lived upstairs. They came down waving American flags at us and told us how glad they were to see us. They wanted to know how to say "thank you," and I told them and then they poured us some wine and we sat around, waiting for the word and drinking the wine.

"If we'd got here nine days sooner," I said, "it would have been the thirtieth anniversary of the British retreat from Mons."

"Who cares?" one of the guys said.

"Nobody cares," I said, "but you don't have to get sore about it."

"Nobody's sore about it," he said. "Just let's fight one war at a time."

"I don't want to fight any of them," I said. "I'll give you both of them."

In about a half hour we moved out. We moved about four miles to a big fieldstone chateau on the left of the road. The general took it over for his CP, and while they were putting the tanks and the half-tracks and the peeps under the trees in the apple orchard in the back, the Belgians were hanging out their flags.

I explained it to the Belgian who owned the place. He was a little guy in long knickers and a tweed jacket and you could see his wealth all over him. I told him who the general was and that we would move out, maybe, the next day. He said he was greatly honored, but I was figuring the mess the tanks would make of his grounds, and what would happen if the Germans should try to bust through the place. At the same time I grabbed a room on the second floor that looked out onto the orchard and had a double bed in it.

We ate under the apple trees. When it started to get dark, I walked back to the chateau, but I stopped to talk to a major I shall call Graves. He had some water in his helmet and he was getting ready to shave, kneeling on the ground with his helmet between his knees, so I took him into the house and up to my room and one of the Belgians brought some hot water. I held my flashlight on his face while he shaved in the mirror over the wash basin, and then we went down and sat around G-2.

They were set up in a den off a library. We sat there listening to the reports coming in until we heard that the first tanks had reached Mons.

"I'd like to go to Mons," I said. I was a war correspondent. "Have we got anything going to Mons?"

"I'll take you to Mons," the major said.

"No," I said. "Why take the chance?"

"If you want to go," the major said.

"No," I said. "If anything is going, I'll go with it."

"C'mon," he said. "We'll go to Mons."

He was a good-looking guy. He was about 6 feet tall, and lean and hard and he had light blue eyes and light brown hair and he was tanned from the sun and the weather.

We went out into the orchard. The moon was up now, and we pulled the branches off his peep and we got in. He gave me the carbine off the dashboard and we drove around the chateau and out onto the road.

It was beautiful in the moonlight. The road was straight, just rolling a little as the country itself rolled. It was lined with poplars and the light breeze was turning the leaves, and the night was all blue and silver.

We rode along, not talking. We passed a couple of American tanks still burning at the side of the road and we knew we were in Mons when we came to the fountain in the middle of the circular grass plot at the head of the main street. We stopped by the fountain and we looked ahead down the street. The street was empty, and there were no lights showing from the houses. There were three Belgians walking around the other side of the fountain, and I called to them and they came halfway around the fountain and stood looking at us.

"Where are the Americans?" I asked.

"There are no Americans," one of them said.

"We might as well drive ahead," I said to the major.

We started down the street. One half of the street was in moonlight, and the other half was in shadow. We drove slowly, the sound of the peep engine and the exhaust the only sound in the street.

"What did they say?" the major asked.

"They said there are no Americans," I said.

"Did they say there are any Germans?" the major asked.

"I didn't ask," I said.

We drove across an intersection and down another block. At the second intersection, the major stopped the peep.

"There's nothing here," he said. "I'd just as soon go back."

"It's all right with me," I said.

He turned the peep around and we drove back through the silent street. We went around the fountain and back down the highway. We drove rapidly now, past the black patches of woods and then the open fields, enjoying the cool of the night and the moonlight. We talked about the silver poplars and about the moon, whether it was a Carolina moon or a Vermont moon, and we were putting the branches back on the peep when a GI came up to the major.

"Excuse me, sir," he said, saluting. "The colonel is looking for you."

"All right," the major said.

He turned to me.

"I'll see you tomorrow."

"You can sleep in the other half of the bed tonight," I said.

"No," the major said. "We're not supposed to sleep in the house."

"You can come up the back stairs," I said.

"All right."

I went up and I went to bed in the clean sheets. About 3 o'clock, I woke up with the firing, and I could sit up in bed and look straight ahead out the window and see the Germans trying to come through the orchard. The whole orchard was growing orange bursts in the darkness and the moonlight, and I reasoned that if they were going to take us, they might as well take me in bed.

In a couple of minutes the firing stopped and I went back to sleep. When I woke up again, the sunlight was coming into the room, and I could hear the GIs talking in the orchard. The major was not there and I figured that it is a funny guy who will take that trip to Mons and who is afraid to sneak up a back stairs against an order.

It was a good day. The sun was warm and the sky was clear and we killed a lot of Germans. They did not know where we were, and they were trying to bust back to the Siegfried Line and they were running into us.

We could stand on the back lawn of the chateau and watch the P-47s work on them. There must have been a column of them trying to cut across in back of us, because we could see the planes peeling off in the blue sky and diving and coming up again from behind a rise of ground, and then we could hear the bomb bursts and see the black smoke rising and the pilots going in with the machine guns.

There was one column that tried to make it across a rise of plowed ground about a quarter of a mile ahead of us. There were a couple of half-tracks and the rest were trucks and there was nothing between us and them but plowed ground. We let them get up onto the rise, and then the 155 Long Toms opened up from a grove just beyond the orchard.

The Long Toms blew them right off the rise of ground. Through glasses we could see some personnel running from the column. They disappeared behind the rise and then came out again where it flattened out, running for some haystacks near a white farmhouse off to the left. There were three of them running in the sunlight over the dry field, our tracers arching at them, orange and slow-looking in the sunlight and kicking up the dust around them.

They ran behind the first haystack, and one of the Long Toms took the haystack. It fired once and the haystack went up in flames, and we stood there watching the haystack burning brightly and never again seeing the Germans who died in the hay.

I walked back across the lawn to the chateau. I started to go into the chateau, but the chaplain, who was a major, came around the side of the building and he called to me. I stopped to talk to him, and he asked if I knew the major I am calling Graves.

"I know him," I said.

"Were you with him last night?"

"Yes."

"Where did you go with him?"

"We took a ride to Mons. We had a nice ride, but we couldn't find anything in the city so we came back."

"After you left him, the colonel sent him back to Mons."

"I knew the colonel was looking for him."

"He wasn't back this morning," the chaplain said, "so we sent a sergeant up the road in an armored peep and he found the major. He was dead by the side of the road and the peep was wrecked. The Germans ambushed him with a machine gun. The machine-gun fire cut the windshield right off the peep, and the Germans took the major's automatic and his field jacket off his body."

I went up to my room in the chateau and I gathered up the major's shaving things and I brought them down and I gave them to the chaplain. I felt very strongly about the major. He had been a strong and confident young officer. We had talked about the moon and the silver of the poplar leaves, and that was important now because it had identified him.

That was one of the strange things about the war, that one death could sometimes make a victory so much less. I was not thinking now about the Germans we were killing but about the American who had been killed. I was wondering about his family and what they were doing and what they were thinking of him now in their not knowing, and I was wondering when they would find out the truth I knew, that their major was dead.

We ate again in the orchard and there was one German sniping us from a patch of woods until a couple of GIs worked around him and flushed him. After we ate, I got a driver and we went down to the prisoner-of-war cage, which was something I did whenever I felt like this. It is a good thing now and then for an Army to see the enemy when he is beaten and dirty and frightened, and around a prisoner-of-war cage the enemy is always weak and so you are always strong.

We had the prisoner-of-war cage back down the road a mile from the chateau. You drove down off the road on the right, and there was an old red-brick sugar refinery there. The trucks kept bringing the prisoners to the refinery, but a lot of prisoners wandered in themselves. All day they kept surrendering, coming across the fields on all sides of us, coming out, when they got hungry or frightened, from the small islands of woods, with their hands on the tops of their heads. By midafternoon we had about 3,000 in the refinery and around it, and when they kept coming in we kept lining them up in the hot, dusty yard for processing, and then we herded them into the refinery to wait for the trucks to come up and take them back.

"This looks like a movie lot," I said to the young second lieutenant who was standing in the yard. "DeMille would like this."

"I never saw so many," the young second lieutenant said.

He was short and dark-haired and a German-American. He had been born in Germany and had lived in America for about seven years before the war started, and he was very proud of his gold bars. He was a serious young second lieutenant, and he was very busy with his job.

"Over here," he was saying, shouting it. "Over here."

They were lining up some new ones, about sixty of them, off a truck. They lined them up in one long line, the prisoners standing with their hands on the tops of their heads, most of them big-eyed and frightened, and the young second lieutenant walked up and down looking at them.

"So!" he said finally, and then shouting it at them in German: "Take everything from your pockets and place it in front of you on the ground."

You could see the panic of the prisoners in their haste to follow the order of the young second lieutenant. They were a long line of men searching their pockets and bending over and straightening up again. When they were finished they stood at attention, their hands stiff at their sides, and the two GIs who had the guard on them went along in front of them, running their hands over each prisoner and then kneeling down in front of him and sorting the knives and razor blades and nail files from the piles.

"So!" the young second lieutenant said. "What is this?"

He was standing in front of a blond, round-faced fat boy who was standing at attention with the others in the line. When he pointed to the ground at the fat boy's feet, the fat boy looked down and blushed and then looked frightened, and those on either side of him looked down at the pile, too, and started to laugh.

"So!" the young second lieutenant said.

The fat boy had spread at his feet a white handkerchief from his pocket. On the handkerchief he had piled some snapshots and a pocketknife, a pocket watch, his identification book and a box of matches. On the top of the pile was a very personal piece of male equipment.

"So!" the young second lieutenant said to him, shouting in German. "You are a lover?"

"*Nein, Herr Hauptmann*," the fat boy said.

He was still blushing, and you could see he was still frightened. On either side of him, the others were laughing softly again.

"Silence!" the young second lieutenant said, looking up and down the line and shouting it at all of them.

The ones on either side of the fat boy stiffened, looking straight ahead again, and the young second lieutenant turned back to the fat boy.

"You will not love for a while," he said.

He turned then and walked down the line. It was clear that the fat boy was the baby and the goat of the regiment, and that the others had never suspected him of anything. Now he seemed very naked, standing and still blushing at attention in the sunlight in the refinery yard.

"Do you want to see something?" the young second lieutenant said to me.

He had walked back, and we had turned and we were walking around the refinery and into the back yard. In the back yard there were about 300 prisoners standing stiffly in double lines, their hands pressed to the sides of their thighs. There were four GIs with clip boards in their hands, interrogating the prisoners and working up and down the lines.

"There is one tough one here," the young second lieutenant said. "Do you want to see him?"

We walked along in front of the prisoners until we came to him. He was the only one in the gray-green, dirty line who had on the black uniform with the red piping of the S.S. tankers, and he was a little taller than the rest. He was handsome, with blond wavy hair and blue eyes, and he stood more stiffly, his head farther back.

"This is an S.S. bastard," the young second lieutenant said, standing in front of the prisoner and looking at the prisoner but talking to me. "He says he is willing to die."

The prisoner stood stiffly, looking over our heads. You could not tell from his face whether he understood English.

"The rest, they tell us everything," the young second lieutenant said. "This one will tell us only his name and his rank and his serial number. He is familiar with the conventions of war."

He looked up at the prisoner's face.

"So!" he said, and now talking in German to the prisoner's face. "You will talk?"

"*Nein*," the prisoner said.

He was still looking over our heads when he said it, and the young second lieutenant turned to the GI standing next to him with the clip board.

"Go get the shovel," he said.

The GI left, and when he came back with the long-handled shovel he handed it to the young second lieutenant and the young second lieutenant handed it to the prisoner, and the prisoner took it. Then the young second lieutenant put the prisoner through a rifle drill with the shovel, the other prisoners standing at attention on both sides of him and behind him, looking straight ahead, their faces stern and not changing.

The prisoner was a good soldier. He was very good following commands with the shovel. The young second lieutenant could see this, and after a minute of it he marched the prisoner out from the ranks of the others and faced him left and had him march, the shovel over his shoulder, to the back of the back yard of the sugar refinery.

There was a wall at the far end off to the right, and the young second lieutenant marched the prisoner toward it. It was a wall of stone and mortar—a good wall—and when the prisoner was about ten feet from the wall the young second lieutenant halted him, and the prisoner stood at attention, facing the direction of the wall.

The GI looked from the young second lieutenant to the prisoner. The GI needed a shave, and he had small brown eyes and he was dirty and obviously tired.

"Sure, Lieutenant," he said. "It'll be a pleasure."

"He is going to dig his grave," the young second lieutenant said. "He is an S.S. bastard."

The GI was still looking at the prisoner, and even when he spoke he did not take his eyes off him."

"It'll be a pleasure," he said, "Lieutenant."

The young second lieutenant walked up to the prisoner. He walked around the prisoner, examining him.

"So!" he said to the prisoner, finally. "Will you talk now?"

"*Nein,*" the prisoner said.

"Would you rather be a living German," the young second lieutenant said, "or a dead German?"

"I will die for the Führer," the prisoner said.

"So!" the young second lieutenant said. "How tall are you?"

"I am six feet," the prisoner said.

"You will dig a hole," the young second lieutenant said, raising his voice and talking right at the prisoner's face again, "seven feet long and three feet wide and three feet deep."

When he said this, he paused for a moment, his face looking up at the prisoner's face, the prisoner at attention, looking off over the young second lieutenant's head, the shovel against his shoulder.

"Dig," the young second lieutenant said.

The prisoner took the shovel off his shoulder. He stood looking at the ground. The ground was covered with black slag and clinkers from the furnaces of the sugar refinery. They had been dumped and spread in the yard for years, and the GI guarding the prisoner was sitting on a pile of them, his Tommy gun still a part of his right arm and resting across one knee, watching the prisoner.

The prisoner worked quickly, but it was slow digging. The black clinkers were hard-packed and, working hard in the hot sun, the prisoner began to perspire. This did not slow the prisoner, however, and he would bend down and drive the shovel into the clinkers and, straightening up, raise it and place the black clinkers carefully in a pile to one side.

He worked hard at this for ten minutes, and then he laid down the shovel and straightened up and took off his tunic. He folded it carefully and laid it on the ground in back of him, and then he went back to the digging. The perspiration was blacker on his black shirt now, and it was wet on the back of his neck and on his face.

"Now will you talk?" the young second lieutenant said to him.

When he spoke to the prisoner, the prisoner straightened up and came to attention, looking out again over the head of the young second lieutenant, the shovel at his side.

"I will die for the Führer," he said.

The young second lieutenant said nothing. He turned and walked over to me and the prisoner resumed his digging.

"He's a tough bastard," the young second lieutenant said to me. "A lot of them are tough bastards."

"He digs," I said, "like he is digging for buried treasure."

"He is a good digger," the young second lieutenant said.

The prisoner had stopped working. He was down about eight or ten inches in the rectangle, and he stepped out of it. He placed the shovel on the ground, and he stood looking at the hole and looking down at himself. Then he stepped into the hole again, and while we watched him he lay down in it. He stiffened his body and with the hard heel of his black boot he made a mark in the cinders. Then he got up, looked at the mark and saw that the hole was plenty long enough, and he picked up the shovel and went on with his digging.

The young second lieutenant walked away toward the sugar refinery, and when he came back again the prisoner had dug down over a foot. It was a neat hole, the corners squared and the walls of it straight, and now the prisoner had dug through the black clinkers and was getting into the hard brown dirt, and the young second lieutenant stood looking at the hole and watching the digging.

"So!" he said finally.

When the young second lieutenant said this, the prisoner climbed out of the hole again and came to attention again in front of the young second lieutenant. Again the shovel was straight at his side and again he looked, his browned face wet and dirty now with sweat, over the head of the young second lieutenant.

"How old are you?" the young second lieutenant said to him.

"I am twenty-two years old," the prisoner said.

"Are you married?"

"*Jawohl.*"

"Have you any children?"

"*Jawohl.*"

"How many children?"

"Two."

"How old are they?"

"I have a son who is four years old," the prisoner said, "and a daughter who is two years old."

"You have a wife and a son and a daughter," the young second lieutenant, saying it quickly and loudly. "Would you like to see them again?"

"*Jawohl.*"

"Will you talk?"

The prisoner's face did not change. He did not move. He just looked over the head of the young second lieutenant, his jaw set, his blue eyes steady.

"I will die for the Führer," he said.

The young second lieutenant looked at me, and then he looked back at the prisoner. I waited for what he would say next, but he turned and I turned with him and we walked back toward the sugar refinery, leaving the prisoner digging under the hot sun, the GI sitting on the pile of black clinkers, the Tommy gun in his lap, another cigaret hanging from his mouth, watching the prisoner.

"What are you going to do?" I said to the young second lieutenant as we walked.

"Nothing."

"You mean you are going to turn him back among these others?"

I pointed toward the yard full of Germans on the two sides of the sugar refinery. There were the long, dirty lines of them with the GIs working up and down the

lines and questioning them, and the young second lieutenant shrugged his shoulders.

"That's right," he said.

"Then maybe you shouldn't have started this," I said.

"What's the difference?" the young second lieutenant
said. "We need a new latrine hole anyway."

After that I did not want to see the end of it, and so I left
him and I drove back to the chateau. When I got back we
were starting to move out. We went up to Mons and
turned right at the fountain in the middle of the circular
grass plot at the head of the street, and that night we got as
far as Charleroi. The next day we made Namur and then
Huy and Liege, and from there we went into Germany.

We saw more of the S.S. after that. The Germans put
a lot of them into their breakthrough in the Ardennes in
December, and once they lined up more than 100 Americans in a field at a crossroad near Malmedy and mowed
them down with a machine gun. The day we dug these
dead Americans out of the snow, the Germans got word
of it and they shelled the field. It did not make the digging any easier.

The next day we took a small Belgian town in a river
valley. There were only a dozen houses in the town and
it was cold and damp in the valley and in front of one of
the houses there was an old Belgian woman sitting in a
rocking chair in the snow. She had on an old housedress
and there was a black shawl around her shoulders. There
was a small bullet hole in her forehead, and she had been
sitting there dead for days because that was the way the
S.S. fought the war and she was a lesson to the town.

In the evenings we did not talk much about the war.
We talked more about what it would be like after the
war. We used to sit around and drink and agree that the
Americans would do a bad job after the war, and one
night we were talking about the S.S. and arguing about

what we could do with them and I told the story about the S.S. tanker and the young second lieutenant in the back yard of the sugar refinery.

"But you have to admit he had guts," one of the others said.

"He had guts," I said, "and at the time I admired it, but it is not so difficult to have guts when you have been trained for it since you were a child."

"Then you think we should have shot him?"

"I will not say that," I said. "I will say only that the mistake we made was in challenging him when he was prepared to go to the end and we were not. It is a mistake we Americans always make in war. They start the game and when we come in we bring our own rules. They play professional rules and we play amateur rules, and so we are always losing a part of the wars we win."

"It's a small thing," the other said. "The main thing is to win the war."

"It is not a small thing," I said. "You were not there and you did not see a Nazi lick us in a back yard of a sugar refinery. You will not be there when we turn him back with his victory into a peacetime Germany. What I saw was the beginning of something, and in a few years you will know what it was."

I knew then that I did not convince them. In their book, Mons was a great victory. It will go that way into the history books, too, because we killed thousands of Germans there and took more than 8,000 prisoners. I knew a major I have called Graves, however, and I saw something in the back yard of a sugar refinery and I said at the time that some day I would write a piece about that thing and, remembering what had happened to the British right there, I would call it "The Retreat at Mons."

The GI's War Fades Away

from *Saturday Evening Post,* 1964

Shortly before six A.M. on December 16, 1944, 17 German divisions, moving through the rain and the fog in the wooded hills of southern Belgium, suddenly struck at four American divisions along an 80-mile front. Here in the mysterious frozen darkness of the Ardennes forests, the Wehrmacht monster turned on its pursuers in one last death struggle. For days the outcome of the fighting was in doubt. Then, after six weeks, this "Battle of the Bulge" was over. It cost 158,000 casualties on both sides. It was the beginning of the end of Hitler's "thousand-year" Reich.

Maubeuge, France

"But why do you wish to see the mayor?" the secretary is saying, and he is a man in his 60's, gray-haired, wearing a dark gray suit.

"Perhaps he can tell me what has happened to the man who was the mayor 20 years ago," I answer.

"It is the same man. Doctor Forest."

I remembered Maubeuge because it was our last French town, and I remembered the mayor because we could not make him understand.

In Maubeuge it was the same as it had been in all the French towns that the Germans evacuated without a fight, and where the people, laughing and crying, throwing flowers and running out with waffles and those bottles of beer with the white-porcelain caps, clogged the streets so that the tanks and half-tracks and the trucks and jeeps could not get through. In all these towns and for all these people the war was over, although it was not over for us, and then I saw the mayor of Maubeuge for the first time.

"What does this man want?" the general was saying, trying to withdraw from the small, excited man who had him by the arm and was trying to pull him from the jeep.

"He's the new mayor," I said. "He wants you to come to the city hall and be honored."

"Tell him we have no time," the general said. There were 30,000 Germans pulling back parallel to us, and if they tried to escape us at Mons we wanted to be there. "Tell him we're trying to fight a war."

As I started to explain to the mayor of Maubeuge, he released his grip on the general's arm and the tank ahead started and the general was gone. It was about four blocks later that I saw the mayor of Maubeuge again, running out of the crowd, and again he had the general by the arm.

"You tried twice to stop the general," I am saying now to the mayor of Maubeuge. "You were wearing a black suit, a black bow tie and a black hat."

"Incredible!" he says now, this small, bald man with the blue-gray eyes, turning to his secretary and his deputy. "It is incredible! After twenty years this man remembers exactly!"

He takes us, then, in his Peugeot and shows us, proudly, the traffic moving past us, the place where he ran up to the general the first time, and he explains that they have changed the road at the corner where he tried a second time. Then we all go to lunch and we toast the memory of the general, for he was killed in another foolish misunderstanding seven months later on a road just south of Paderborn, Germany.

It was dusk when the German Tiger tank cut off his jeep and, as he tried to surrender his automatic and reached for it, a kid in the turret and just out of Panzer school cut him down. This ended, at 46 years, the life of Major General Maurice Rose.

"The General Rose was a great general, yes?" the mayor of Maubeuge is saying.

"Yes," I say. "He was as fine a tank commander as we had in the American Army."

"He was a brave man," the mayor of Maubeuge says.

The mayor of Maubeuge and his secretary and his deputy are brave men too. They headed the local Resistance, and they still get letters from American fliers they sheltered and moved through the Underground, and so I do not tell them what the general told me, when the mayor of Maubeuge had him by the arm the second time.

"Tell this man for the last time that we're fighting a war," the general said, angry and his face hard. *"Tell him that if he doesn't get off this vehicle I'll shoot him."*

It was just a misunderstanding.

Mons, Belgium

We crossed the Belgian border at 4:10 that afternoon with our lead tanks pushing to take the high ground just west of Mons. The road is absolutely straight and where it widens out now for the Customs it was then just the blacktop ending and the beginning of the two-lane concrete. In the cul-

*vert that runs under the road just inside Belgium a woman
and her two small daughters were hiding, and now the
woman has been dead for four years and the daughters are
married and have moved away.*

The little man who owned the big fieldstone-and-red-
brick château about two miles up on the left side of the
road is dead, too, but his widow still lives there with a
son and a daughter and their families. She is a stout
woman who uses a hearing aid, and she talks about the
general as if he spent the whole war there instead of just
two days and two nights.

"He was charming," she keeps saying. "The General
Rose stayed right here and I was enchanted."

*Her husband kept saying, too, how honored he was.
While he was running around in those long knickers and
tweed jacket and looking like a lot of money, he kept saying
it, and I kept thinking of the mess our tanks would make of
his orchard and wondering what would happen if the Germans should try to break through this place.*

"You remember," I say now, "that we ate our meals here
behind the cover of this grove?"

"Yes," George Hicks says. Twenty years ago he was a
war correspondent for the National Broadcasting Company. We have come back together. "The first day at lunch
a sniper kept trying to pick somebody off, and everybody
was spilling his coffee and getting madder by the minute
until a couple of GI's went out and flushed him."

"And I remember," I say, "how innocent he looked—
just a kid—when they marched him back here with his
hands on the top of his head."

It is still plowed ground just beyond the grove and for
as far as you can see. About a quarter of a mile from the

grove the plowed ground crests, and where the tractor is working the crest now, the dust rising from it, the column of Germans tried to come.

They came from the left, a couple of armored half-tracks and the rest trucks, and it was just high noon. There was nothing between them and us but this quarter of a mile of plowed ground and they had no idea we were here, and our people just let them come. They let them get up onto the crest, strung out in that single line, and then, from the trees just beyond the orchard, the 155-mm Long Toms opened up. The Long Toms worked from the ends toward the middle and there were pieces of trucks and pieces of half-tracks and pieces of people just flying through the air.

"And then," I am saying, "do you remember the Germans running?

"Yes," George Hicks says. "There were three of them and they ran to the left there, where those two haystacks are standing again."

Somehow they had got out of that column, and they were running as hard as they could. For a moment they disappeared behind the rise and then they came out again, still running, where it flattens out, and we watched our tracers arching at them, orange and slow-looking in the sunlight, and kicking up the dust. They ran behind the first haystack, and when they did, one of our Long Toms took the haystack. It fired once and the haystack went up in flames, and we stood here watching the haystack burning brightly and never again seeing the three Germans who died in the hay.

It was when I walked away from that that I met the chaplain. He asked me if I knew the mayor I shall call Graves.

"Yes," I said. "I know him."

I had met him the evening before. It was just getting dark and he was in the orchard. He had some water in his helmet, and he was kneeling with the helmet between his knees and getting ready to shave. I took him instead up to my room with the big double bed in it on the second floor of the château and got him some hot water and held my flashlight on his face while he shaved in the mirror over the washbasin.

Later we were sitting around G-2 in the big square room with the white-marble floor and the grand piano in one corner and the chandelier made of deer antlers when we heard that the first American tanks were in Mons. The major was in his late 20's, slim and good-looking with light-brown hair and blue eyes, and he asked me if I wanted to go to Mons. I said the first Belgian city would be a story, if we could manage to get in, and then he said he would take me to Mons.

He said it just like that, and we went out into the orchard and took the branches off his jeep, and he took the carbine off the dashboard and put it between the seats. Then we moved out into the moonlight and we drove to Mons. The moonlight was very bright and like snow on the fields and the road, except where the dark patches of woods came down to the road, and where the poplars bordered the road a light breeze was stirring their leaves and turning them silver in the moonlight.

We did not talk as we rode. We passed a couple of American tanks still burning at the side of the road, and we knew we were in Mons when we came to the statue in the middle of the circular grass plot. We stopped by the statue and then went around it and down the street. One half of the street was in moonlight and the other half was in shadow, and the sound of the jeep engine and of the exhaust was the only sound in the street. When we found no Americans in Mons we turned around and on the way back we talked.

"After you got back," the chaplain said that next noon, "the colonel sent the major back to Mons."

"I knew the colonel was looking for him," I said.

While we were putting the branches back over the jeep a GI had come up and had given him the message. Then we had walked to the château together and I had told the major that, when he got back, he could sleep in the other half of the bed if he wanted to.

"No," the major said. "We're not supposed to sleep in the house."

"You can come up the back stairs," I said.

"All right."

I went up and went to bed in the clean sheets. About three o'clock I woke up with the firing, and I could sit up in the bed and look straight ahead out of the leaded-glass window and see the Germans trying to come through the orchard. The whole orchard was growing orange bursts in the darkness and the moonlight, and after it stopped I went back to sleep. When I woke up again the sunlight was coming into the room and I could hear GI's talking in the orchard and the major was not there and no one had slept in the other half of the bed.

"When Major Graves wasn't back this morning," the chaplain said, "they sent a sergeant up the road in an armored jeep."

"Oh," I said, and I knew before he said it. I had thought it first when I had awakened and now I knew.

"The sergeant found the major," the chaplain said. "He was dead by the side of the road and the jeep was wrecked. The Germans ambushed him with a machine gun. The machine gun cut the windshield right off the jeep, and the Germans took the major's automatic and his field jacket off his body."

I went up to the room in the château and I gathered up the major's shaving things, and I brought them down and I gave them to the chaplain. Then I got a jeep and a driver and we went back down the road about a mile to the old red-brick sugar refinery where they had the prisoner-of-war cage. I thought that looking at some German prisoners would make me feel better.

They had plenty of prisoners to look at. They had 3,000 of them in the refinery and around it. They had three German generals and 12 ambulances. In one of the ambulances there was a dead German and a motorcycle, and in the others there were cans of sardines and bars of soap and blankets and surgical instruments and boots and canteens and newspapers and those hard, flat biscuits, and bandages and cotton and Christmas cards.

"But there is no one buried in the yard," the director of the refinery, a stocky, middle-aged man, whose name is Maton, is saying now. "There are no Germans buried here."

"I know," I say, "but I would like to find the place where I watched the young S.S. tanker dig his own grave."

"If you wish," he says. "We can examine the yard."

The S.S. tanker had refused to talk. The rest of them, the officers excepted, were all talking, but the S.S. tanker had said he was willing to die. He was a good-looking blond, but arrogant like all the S.S. When we ordered him to start digging his own grave because we said we were going to shoot him if he didn't talk, he got down and measured his length on the ground and then dug a grave, sweating in the hot sun and from the effort of getting through the earth.

"It was right over there," I am saying, pointing to where a poured-concrete wall now has been erected to hold refuse from the furnaces.

"Perhaps," the director says, "but there is no grave there."

"I know," I say. I know because they never did break him.

*When the young second lieutenant who was doing the
questioning asked him, he said he had a wife and two small
children back in Germany, but when the young lieutenant
tried to work on that the young S.S. tanker still said he was
willing to die for his Führer.*

*"So what are you going to do?" I said when we walked
away.*

"Nothing," the young second lieutenant said.

*"You mean you are going to let him get away with this in
front of all the others?"*

"That's right."

"Then you shouldn't have gotten into this."

*"We need a new latrine hole anyway," the young second
lieutenant said.*

*I rode back then to the château thinking about the major
and the S.S. tanker. In three days at Mons the 3rd Armored
Division captured 9,000 Germans, and the 1st Infantry Division in support captured 17,000.*

"But you weren't disturbed?" I am saying to the stout
widow with the hearing aid, sitting under the chandelier
made of deer antlers. "You were not bothered by the
damage done to your grounds and your orchard?"

"Oh, no," she says, smiling. "Only an American soldier took the carved lion's head from the newel post of
the stairway."

Liége, Belgium

*We went in that morning with the Combat Command that
had swung around to the right and came up from the southeast and along the right bank of the Meuse. There was very
little fighting in the city as the Germans withdrew and we
wrote our stories in the first bar we came to. We had only a
half hour to write them to get them back to the Cub plane*

that would fly them out, and up at the end of the block the first tank was firing into a corner building. A half hour later the street was filled with people waving homemade American flags, and all the way through the city it was that way, the first two or three tanks and then the people spilling out behind them with their joy and with the flags and marking the progress of the advance.

"But why do you wish to visit the basement now?" the *chef de bureau* is saying. He is short and big in the chest and he looks you right in the face because, like all good office managers, he wants answers.

The Hôpital de Bavière is on the other side of the Meuse and north of the center of the city. It is a walled complex of old red-brick buildings, and when we went in there, the three of us, dirty and tired, the Sisters of the Order of Augustine de Bavière in their white robes with the black coif brought us pails of hot water and poured them into the white tub that stood in the center of the room.

"Now may I ask of you a favor?" the one called Sister Eugénie said after I had bathed and shaved, and her face, framed, oval and soft and starting to age, had the beauty of a painting. "Before the fighting for the city, we moved our sick outside of the city. The ones we could not move because they are too ill are still here. They are two hundred and they are in the basement. For two days they have heard the guns and have waited for this moment of liberation and now they ask to see an American."

"But I am only a writer," I said. "I did not liberate them. The first American they should see should be an American soldier."

I went out onto the street, but the one GI I found said he didn't think he would be good at it, and so I went back and Sister Eugénie led me down the curved stone stairway. At the foot of the stairway there was a naked light bulb hanging

*from the ceiling and, as we stopped under the bulb, I could
see, in the weak light of the other bulbs down the long, gray
corridor the sick, the too sick to be moved. They were lying
on mattresses on the floor along both sides of the corridor, all
of them facing us, and they had heard the sound of our feet
coming down the stairway, and there was silence and the
faces staring. Then Sister Eugénie said one thing.*

"This," she said, "is an American."

*The first one was an old man and, as I stopped and bent
over, he reached up his arms and, as I bent down, he pulled me
to my knees. The bones of his thin arms were hard across the
back of my neck, the stubble of beard rough against my cheek,
the bones of his face hard against my face with his tears between. He did not want to let me go, the two of us shaking as
one with his sobs, and Sister Eugénie knelt down and slowly
opened his arms and I went on, walking, with them reaching
to touch my clothing because I was an American.*

"But there are no sick there now," the *chef de bureau* is
saying, "and Sister Eugénie died in 1960."

"I know," I say.

"It is all changed there now. There are laboratories
and offices and the workshop for the electrician and the
plumber."

"I understand."

"Then why do you want to go? You would not find it
the same there now."

Leading into the city from the south there is one
street with the Vesdre River on the right and, at one
point, a brick wall on the left. On the brick wall, painted
in yellow letters, are the words: YANKES ASSASSINS.
It is Communist propaganda against NATO and no one
has painted it out.

*When we came into the city 20 years ago they kept apolo-
gizing for the homemade American flags. Some were just*

*crayoned on paper and some of the cloth ones had no stars
in the blue field and one had polka dots for stars and not
enough of them.*

*"But we are so sorry not to be ready with your flag," one
woman said, crying. "We did not expect you for two more
days."*

Eilendorf, Germany

*It was about 10 o'clock at night, and quiet in the cellar ex-
cept for the occasional artillery outside. The ones that were
close sounded like two big pieces of lumber being clapped together, and each time one went off like that it would rattle
the door leading out to the back of what was left of the house.*

*"You know this house has taken twelve direct hits?" the
captain said. "But I'll tell you something else."*

*There were four of us in the cellar, and we had only a
half bottle of whiskey, so it wasn't that. It was that the
captain had had his company up on this ridge now for 39
days and 39 nights. The ridge is two miles northeast of
Aachen, and the 1st Infantry Division put two companies
on the ridge before it went into Aachen to take the first
German city slowly, house by house and block by block.
The two companies kept turning back the Germans who
were trying to relieve their people in Aachen, and it had
been very bad.*

"This is an American journalist," the interpreter is saying now to the woman in the doorway of the house. "He
was here, in your cellar, twenty years ago, and he wonders now if you will allow him to see your cellar again."

The woman is short and plump and middle-aged, and
she has on a dark-blue housedress and blue bedroom slippers. She has plastic curlers in her hair, red and orange

and blue and green and yellow curlers, and she looks at me and then back at the interpreter."

"She says," the interpreter says, "that she is eating. She asks us to come back in a half hour."

"Then she'll let us in?"

"Why not?"

"She's not mad that we knocked her house apart, although it was the Germans who really did it?"

"She has only been living here a few years," the interpreter says. "A farmer lived here when you were here."

The captain was six feet two and he had lost 25 of his 170 pounds. He was sitting at the table with the lighted candle on it and the map and the two field phones in the light-brown leather cases. The lieutenant was sitting backward on the straight-backed chair, his arms folded across the top of the back and his chin on his arms, and he and Gordon Fraser of NBC and I formed a kind of semicircle around the table and the captain.

"But I'll tell you something else," the captain said. He said it slowly. "You know why this candle burns here? Because out here on this ridge, starting 50 yards from here, there are kids who have nothing, except wet and cold and shelling and misery and the Germans coming at them, and they're dying."

We took three major attacks here, the captain said, battalion strength or better, and in the first one, he said, I lost every man in my second squad of my first platoon. They weren't wounded, he said. They weren't captured, he said. They were killed, he said, but we piled them up. One German reached a heavy machine gun, he said, and fell dead right over it. When they reached our mortar positions, he said, there was a kid who was hit, and he waited until the German showed himself, and then he shot him and the Ger-

man toppled over and they died side by side, the captain said, and we really piled them up.

We literally piled them up, he said, at least 70 of them, and after we counterattacked, he said, there were over 200 bodies for 18 of ours spread over 400 yards. And the kids, he said, they don't want them moved. He said they stink, but the kids say they can live with the stink because they don't think the Germans will come over their dead. And for 17 consecutive days, he said, we were shelled with a minimum of 500 rounds a day and we still annihilated three waves of infantry, he said.

"She says we may come in now," the interpreter is saying. "Her name is Nyssen, and her husband is a chauffeur and they moved here from Aachen."

The woman has taken the curlers out of her hair, and she has put on black shoes, and she leads us through the small white kitchen and we go down the cellar stairs. The room is about the right size, but the ceiling is too low. I don't remember that the ceiling was this low.

"Oh, she says the ceiling is new," the interpreter says. "She says they had to put in a new ceiling and new floor."

The cellar floor is black with the dust of the briquettes and the small coal piled in the corner where I slept. Against the wall where the table was there are shelves, and on them are empty wine bottles and fruit jars and three empty Bols pints and a crate of green pears.

"So that's the way it is," the captain was saying. "They say, 'OK, I'll get the water for the platoon,' and they start out and they're blown to bits right here outside that door where you came in.

"They don't come off here with flesh wounds," he said. "They come off here with legs gone and arms gone, with

their eyes shot out, with jaws gone, with their guts gone. They come off here dead.

"And one of them comes to me," he said, "and he says, 'I can't take it any more.' And I say, 'You will.' He says, 'But captain, I can't.' And I grab him by the throat and I shake him and I say, 'You will. If I lose you I lose a squad. If I lose a squad, I lose a platoon. If I lose a platoon, we lose this ridge, and we're not gonna lose this ridge. There's no going back from this ridge, except dead.' Then I turn him around and he goes out and I watch and a mortar comes in and he's dead.

"I've lost 112 out of 136," he said, "but we took our goddamn ridge and we're holding it, aren't we?"

He was looking right at Gordon Fraser.

"Yes," Fraser said.

"And we took your Omaha Beach, didn't we?" he said, looking at me.

"Yes."

"And we broke through and we chased the goddamn Germans across France and Belgium and we came up here . . . "

He stopped and I could see it coming.

". . . and we died," he said. "We died right here, because they'll never be another G Company like this one. Never."

And then he cried. The big gaunt man put his head in his hands and he cried. I could hear, outside, the shelling, then a machine gun fired one burst somewhere and then, in the silence of the room, because the captain was crying quietly, I was aware for the first time that a small battery radio was playing at the end of the table against the wall, and that Lily Pons was singing.

"Shut up," the captain said.

No one had said anything, but the captain had raised his head from his hands and he was listening.

"The 'Bell Song' from Lakmé," *he said. "Puccini."*

"No," the lieutenant said. "Not Puccini, but I can't remember the name of the guy."

Months later after I was home again I looked it up and, of course, Delibes wrote it. The captain was Joe Dawson and we named the ridge after him.

"But if they are going to take a photograph of my cellar," Frau Nyssen is saying, "I must clean it."

"No!" John Launois, who is taking the pictures, says. "Tell her, 'No!' Tell her not to touch a thing."

"But in America," Frau Nyssen is saying, "the people will think that I don't keep my house well."

Aachen, Germany

It was the same in all the cities where they held out and fought house to house. First we put the air on them and then the artillery, and the fronts of the houses just fell out into the streets. It was the start of the autumn rains when the infantry took Aachen, so the hills of rubble, wet by the rain, smelled of plaster and charred wood and of the disintegrating bodies underneath. The infantry, running low and spaced out, preferred building lines and doorways for cover, and the rubble forced them out into the middle of the streets.

"Somewhere in this city," I say to Dr. Fritz Velz, who is the head of the tourist-and-information bureau, "there is a domed plaster ceiling, and on it are painted pink cherubs floating amid white clouds in a blue sky."

"I don't know," Doctor Velz says. "You must find that?"

"Yes."

Doctor Velz is semi-stout and he has long, almost straight white hair and a ruddy complexion.

"Doctor Velz," the interpreter says, "wants everything to your satisfaction. He will inquire about the ceiling."

Eighty-three percent of the houses were destroyed or damaged in Aachen and 70 churches and 50 schools. In what was left of the houses there were canaries dead in their cages and rubber plants turning yellow and, in the kitchens and dining rooms, where the chairs had been pushed away from the tables in haste, the food had turned to mold on the plates. At the foot of a child's bed, sitting so that it faced toward the pillow at the other end, was a doll with its arms outstretched. There were also the Nazi propaganda books and swastika armbands and swastika pins.

"Ah, yes," Doctor Velz says when he comes back. "That ceiling is in the Suermondt-Museum. That was where the American Military Government had its headquarters. You wish to go there now?"

The lieutenant colonel who was the head of the American Military Government was very worried about the whole ceremony. He said we absolutely had to find somebody who would serve as bürgermeister if we were going to get Aachen running again. He said out of 10,000 civilians he had managed to get 12 names, and five had said they might serve, but they were all afraid of Nazi reprisals, and now he had picked one.

"Yes," I say now. "This is it. This is the ceiling."

"But this was not a library then," the director, Dr. Gunther Grimme, is saying. The museum specializes in the Netherlands School of the fifteenth and sixteenth centuries and in sculpture on the Middle Ages, and the most prized of its possessions is Rubens's *Damnation*.

The lawyer was 43 years of age and his name was Franz Oppenhoff, and he stood under the domed ceiling with the cherubs on it. He was rather short, and balding, with an oval face, and he had on a gray-herringbone topcoat.

"Although a bürgermeister can be instituted even against his will," the lieutenant colonel said, "no amount of coercion can make him serve. Therefore you gentlemen of the press will not be able to use this man's name. Also photographers will not be permitted to take his picture."

The lawyer was standing with his back to us. The lieutenant colonel swore the lawyer in that way, with an American Bible, and then, without turning to look at us or saying anything, the lawyer walked out.

"He can be a great help to us," the lieutenant colonel said, "if he lives."

There is a 12-foot-high bas-relief of the Crucifixion on an outside wall of the St. Nicholas Church, and 20 years ago somebody sprayed it with a machine gun. There are chips out of the right shin of the Christ and a finger is missing from His left hand, and one of the apostles is without a head, but there is very little evidence of the war in Aachen now. They moved three million cubic yards of rubble, and the fountain with the colored lights at the start of the Autobahn to Cologne is like a roulette wheel with the traffic spinning around it. On Charlemagne's throne in the Imperial Cathedral 32 rulers were crowned, and there is the municipal theater and the technological university and the thermal baths and the annual horse show.

"We talked of what they wanted him to do," Mrs. Oppenhoff is saying, "but it was clear that my husband had to do it for his country and for his city."

She is a rather small, gracious woman who looks younger than her years. Her gray hair is set in small curls, and she is wearing a black skirt and a white blouse.

"It was the evening of Palm Sunday," she says. "They had come down in the woods by parachute. We were at a neighbor's house, and the maid came and said she thought that some Americans wanted to talk to my husband. He came here, and they were Nazi youth, and they shot him by the door leading out to the garden.

"The trial was in 1949," she says. "Three of them were sentenced, but they did not get hard punishments. They have never found the one that, the others say, was the killer. My husband had told me that we had to do, both of us, a great sacrifice, but I couldn't have known, of course, that the sacrifice would be that great."

They named a street after her husband. They changed the name of Kaiseralle to Oppenhoffallee.

Werth, Germany

There was nothing moving in the town, so we parked the jeep behind the yellow fieldstone back wall which was all that was standing of the first house on the left and, in the bright afternoon sunlight, we walked down the sloping dirt road into the center of the town. There were only about three dozen houses in the town, and they were all of yellow fieldstone and they had all been hit, although the small, red-brick church was still standing.

The church stood at the right of the only intersection, and there was a shell hole in the roof and another shell hole in the wall at window height almost big enough to crawl through. When I looked through the shell hole, I could see the wooden benches that had been tossed around and broken, but the altar, with the clean white lace cloth on it, was intact. At the right side of the altar there was a life-size, painted plaster statue of the Savior, with His right hand extended. On the left of the altar there was a similar figure of the Virgin with the head, lying on its right side,

at the feet. About 10 feet down the aisle there was an un-
exploded 150-mm shell, and another 10 feet beyond the
shell a dead German soldier was lying face down, his feet
toward the altar. He was wearing a black helmet, with a
narrow orange band painted around it, and he had his full
field pack strapped to his back. I could tell he had been shot
while running, because his left foot was still crossed be-
hind the calf of his right leg, the way he had tripped as he
had fallen.

Up the dirt road to the left, where the houses ended, there
was one of our medium tanks parked behind a high green
hedge. Fifty yards beyond it there was a broken yellow-
fieldstone farmhouse, and there were three GI's in it looking
out of the window at a .50-caliber machine gun about 70
yards out on the slope of the green field. They had aban-
doned the gun when the Germans had caught them in a
cross fire, and they were debating whether to make a run to
recover the gun or whether to wait for darkness. They were
all afraid of their captain, but they were more afraid of the
Germans, so I finally left them and started back toward the
intersection. Where the medium tank was parked by the
hedge, there were two GI's standing and looking down at
another GI who was lying between the road and the hedge.
He was lying on his back in the sunlight, a khaki blanket
over him with just his head and his feet showing.

"Maybe he's asleep," one of the GI's was saying.

"Asleep, hell," the other said. "Can't you see he's dead?"

At the intersection the Germans had been throwing in
some mortars, and the GI's were standing in the doorways.
When I passed the church I looked through the shell hole
again, and the dead German was still there. He was still
sprawled out in the aisle, in his gray-green uniform and
black helmet with the orange stripe, and his full field pack
and his left foot crossed behind the calf of his right leg. At
the altar two GI's were kneeling and praying.

"He says," the interpreter is saying, "that this was not his parish during the war. His parish was at Untermaubach, just south of Düren, but he came here right after the war. He says 90 percent of this village was destroyed."

"I know," I say.

The priest is short and stocky with black hair and heavy black eyebrows, and dark eyes. In his black-felt hat he reminds me of Fiorello La Guardia.

"He says the church is all new now. They have been rebuilding it for 15 years, and last Christmas they received the organ and the bells."

It is gray stucco now and modern, and the roads that run past it are no longer dirt but blacktop. All of the houses are stucco now, except for the farmhouse where the GI's debated about the machine gun, and from one of the houses across the street we can hear men's voices singing and then laughing.

"He says," the interpreter says, "that they have won their football match, but about his church, he says it is not a large one and he is curious why you from America are interested in it."

"Tell him," I say, "that, during the war, I looked through a shell hole into his church and I want him to know that, at his altar, two American soldiers were praying."

I watch him, listening to the interpreter. I watch his eyes, and then he starts to talk, and I see his eyes fill.

"He says," the interpreter says, "that in Untermaubach there were American Negro soldiers who were prisoners. He says he still tells the people in his parish about them. He says that whenever he walked through the village, carrying the Body and Blood of Christ to the sick, the American Negroes would kneel in the street. He says he tells them that here many of them do not even lift their hats."

"Thank him for me," I say. "Thank him very much."

I do not tell him about the German soldier I saw sprawled in the aisle of his church, dead because he, too, had stopped to pray.

Übach-Palenberg, Germany

It was almost dark and raining hard, and on the right the infantry was moving up, in a long, curving line, moving into the rain and onto the big, flat plain. Where the plain ended, the ground dropped away, and there was only the darkening gray sky with the artillery bursts like sunflowers against it. The bursts lighted the faces of the infantry and gleamed on their helmets and rifles and wet clothing, and as the infantry walked toward the bursts and the head of the long, curving line reached the end of the plain and disappeared, it seemed as if they were walking off the end of the world. It was the 30th Division and they were going to have to go through the Siegfried Line and attack the next town.

"There it is," I am saying, pointing toward the broken slabs of concrete on the grassy knoll next to the parking space and across the street from the small hotel. "Our infantry came across the railroad tracks here and it was getting toward night and raining hard, and this was the first pillbox they took."

There is a wooden soft-drink stand between the pillbox and the street now, and a board fence runs between the soft-drink stand and the restaurant. Next to the restaurant there is a grocery store, and they are both owned by a couple of brothers named Joeris. Paul Joeris is 35 years old, and he has gold caps on his canine teeth, and blond hair and blue eyes, and he is wearing gray slacks and a brown sport jacket, and his sport shirt is open at the neck.

"So you're the one who shot everything up here?" he says, but he is smiling.

"We and your own people," I say. "Your own people did the most damage after we got in here."

"No matter," he says, shrugging. "I was only a boy then."

The GI's blew the outer steel door off the pillbox with a bazooka, and inside they found three wounded Germans and a dead German. They also found a phonograph and some records, three typewriters, a half dozen cameras and a lot of pink lingerie. The GI's had a lot of fun with the lingerie, holding it up in front of themselves in the candlelight and, with the rain and the artillery falling outside, sashaying around the three rooms. The captain made no objection to it, but it was obvious he didn't see much humor in it and that he was getting morose.

"You train and train with guys," he said at one point, "and three months later you look around and where are they? They're all gone. All the good guys are gone. The sergeant and I are pinned down in a hole, and when it lets up I shake him and say, 'C'mon. C'mon. Let's get goin'.' He can't get goin'. He's dead. Will you tell me what the hell I'm being saved for?"

"For the Pacific," somebody said.

It could have been the artillery that was getting the captain. It was really shaking the ground and, although it was safe enough in the pillbox, the captain knew that the next morning they would have to clean out the Germans who were spotting for the artillery and sniping from the slag heap 100 yards up the road.

"You see," Paul Joeris is saying now. "It is impossible to enter."

The way the roof was blown, it has fallen into the pillbox. There is a mulberry tree, the trunk about as big around as a man's forearm, growing at what had been the entrance, and as far as you can see in, there is refuse, old papers, cartons, broken eggshells; orange peels and a rusty length of pipe.

"We young Germans," Paul Joeris says, "use these things for garbage."

"But he has been telling me," the interpreter says, "that he is thinking of buying this property to put a large store on it. Before he buys he must know exactly where the foundations of the pillbox go. They get what would be in American money $6,250 from the government to get rid of these pillboxes, but he says that if the foundation wall is there it will cost too much. He wants you to remember it as exactly as you can."

"Well," I say, "it was a big one. The entrance was here, and there was one room here and another room here, and the message center was at the other side. It slept 24 men in triple-decker bunks, if they could sleep."

The captain slept well, although I couldn't sleep. The shelling made too much noise, and the air was so stagnant that I had to get up every half hour and turn the iron crank on the ventilator for 10 or 15 minutes. The next morning, though, the captain felt much better, especially when we heard our tanks coming across the railroad tracks and up the street, because the tanks would get the Germans out of the slag pile.

"Then, if that is true," Joeris says, "the foundation must run all the way to the street."

"That's right."

The tanks started the Germans shelling again, but finally I went out to try to find our driver. He was a black-haired, blue-eyed Irishman and he was the best driver in the press camp. He was also the best looter I ever saw. He had pulled

*the jeep with the trailer around so that it was pointing
down the street and out of town, and then I saw him, coming around the corner. He was riding a bike and over one
arm he had about a dozen women's dresses, on their hang-
ers, and first he put the bicycle into the trailer and the
dresses on top of it.*

*"Hey, Mac!" One of the kids was calling to him from a
doorway because they were still shelling. "Don't you know
you ain't supposed to loot?"*

"Yeah," he said, still loading the trailer. "I heard."

*What the kid didn't know was that he would loot any-
thing. Before the war he had been a truck driver, and he was
saving up to buy a whole fleet of trucks when he got home.
Once he even looted a girl. She was a Dutch girl, and he
brought her back to the press camp dressed in a GI overcoat
and helmet. He said she was very refined, and he hoped to
marry her and loot her all the way back to the U.S. He said
she played the piano. The way he put it was that she played
Chopin without even reading the music, and he said he and
the girl's mother sat one whole evening just listening to her
play it.*

"Then, if you're right," Joeris is saying, "that's no good."

"He says," the interpreter says, "that if you're right it
will cost him too much money and he can't buy the
property."

"I'm sorry," I say. "I wish him luck, but I didn't expect
to come back here 20 years later as a real-estate ap-
praiser."

*Our driver never did loot the very refined girl all the way
back to the U.S., though. One day he came and told me, his
head hanging a little, that he had had to go and see the
medics. He was the only one I ever heard of who got it listening to Chopin.*

Inden, Germany

The infantry company was from the 104th Division, and two thirds of them were in the three rooms of the cellar on the edge of the mile of open ground. The mile of open ground was all that separated them from the Germans in the next town, but it was a fine cellar.

It obviously had been built as a shelter, with a heavy, arched ceiling, and along one wall in each room there was a wide, slightly sloping shelf, for sleeping, and covered with straw. It was about 11 o'clock at night and the Germans were shelling heavily, and at eight o'clock the next morning the infantry would have to climb up out of the cellar and go across the open ground.

"He says there's no one in the police station," the interpreter is saying. "He is the only policeman in the town."

He is sitting on his motorcycle at the head of the driveway. He looks about 30 years of age, well-built, with a square face and strong neck and brown eyes. He is wearing a white plastic helmet and a green leather jacket and green trousers.

"He says he wasn't here during the war. He doesn't know of any cellar that was a shelter and near a bridge, but he is willing to lead us through the town."

When the men got to sleep it was quiet in the cellar, except for the constant shelling, muffled by the heavy walls and ceiling, and for the sounds that the men made in their sleep. Every now and then one of them would say something in his sleep, or cry out, and then I was conscious of one of them talking.

"Wake that man," the captain said, and I had thought that he had been asleep too. "He's talking in his sleep."

"No, he's not, sir," a voice said at the far end of the room. "He's awake, sir."

"What's the matter with him?"

"He says it's his eyes, sir. He says his eyes are burning, and something about a gun."

"Take him to a medic," the captain said.

Then it was quiet again, and then I heard the stirring again at the far end of the room. In the candlelight I could see the two GI's, the GI in back with his hands on the shoulders of the one in front, guiding the other between the men sleeping in the straw.

"Now if he steps on you guys," the GI in back said, "don't say anything. If stumbles over you, don't get mad."

"What's the matter with him?" one of them, lying in the straw, said.

"He can't see," the GI said.

After that there was just the muffled sound of the shelling, the sounds of the men breathing heavily and turning in their sleep, and the taffeta sound of the straw.

"Well," the interpreter is saying, "is it the cellar?"

"I don't know," I say. "I'm not sure."

"But it has the arched ceiling."

"Yes."

"She says she would like to know someone who stayed in her cellar," the interpreter says, meaning the woman who owns the house. The woman is middle-aged, with dark-brown hair, and she is wearing a dark blue dress and smiling at us. "She says she wants it very much to be the right cellar."

"I would like it to be the right cellar too," I say, "but the rooms seemed bigger. I can't place all of us here."

"And she says they closed off one room when they rebuilt the house."

"It may be," I said.

It was five minutes before the attack across the open ground when the GI shot himself. There was the quick report and a small orange flame, and at first I thought a shell had hit right over the cellar. Then the GI was rolling at our feet on the straw, holding his hand and moaning.

"What's this wire doing here?" the captain said.

The GI had worked it out during the night while the rest were sleeping, and it was obvious how he had done it. He had placed his rifle upright on the small table and leaned it against the wall. Then he had taken a wire from a crate of K rations and wrapped one end around one of the legs of the table. He had hooked the other end over the trigger of his rifle. Then he had picked up the rifle with his right hand, his left hand over the end of the barrel, and the bullet had gone through the thick of his left hand.

"I don't know anything about a wire," he was saying, moaning and rolling on the straw.

The wire was supposed to fall down out of sight, but it didn't. It was sticking straight up, the end still hooked, and the whole two thirds of the company in the cellar filed past the wire and up the stairs and into the shelling and out across the mile of open ground.

"If it is not that cellar," the interpreter is saying, and we are standing outside and looking at the two-story white-stucco house now, "the officer says there are no others like it. He says, anyway, that he must go now for his exercise."

"His exercise?" I say, and I notice for the first time that his green trousers are really sweatpants, and his shoes are black-leather gym shoes with rubber soles.

"Every year he has to take a physical examination. This is the afternoon each week that he takes his exercise."

"But it was a red-brick house," I say.

"The lady says that this house was red brick during the war, but then it was so much destroyed they built it this way."

"But I remember that above the cellar there was just one corner of two walls remaining, and in that corner a refrigerator was standing."

"Yes," the interpreter says, "she says that there was a white refrigerator standing just as you say. It is not your cellar?"

"I don't know," I say. "This street was so different."

"This does not look like the street?"

The street was half-filled with rubble, and there was a Sherman tank parked behind one wall. The shelling was so intense that the tankers were down in the cellar of the house, with the line to their headset running from the tank through the cellar window.

"Get out of there!" one of the tankers was hollering at us from the window. "You guys better get out of there!"

Gordon Fraser was trying to turn the jeep around, but the single knuckle joint of the trailer hitch was giving him trouble, and the trailer kept doubling back. When he got it around, the two left wheels were up on a pile of rubble, so that the jeep was canted over to the right, and then it stalled. There was a dead German, just his shoulders and arms and his helmeted head protruding, wedged between the right front fender and the wheel.

"What's the matter?" Fraser was hollering.

"There's a dead German wedged between the right front fender and wheel," I was hollering.

"Well, pull him out."

"I can't," I was hollering. "Put it in the low gear."

So he put it in the low gear and the jeep started, the head and shoulders of the dead German shaking and the arms flopping. When I got into the jeep and we started down the street, there were a dozen Germans coming up the street, their hands on their helmets, and they had seen it all.

"I don't know if it looks like the street or not," I am saying.

"Then the officer must go for his exercise," the interpreter says.

Hürtgen, Germany

The Hürtgen Forest was the worst of it all. The fir trees were 60 feet tall and planted 10 feet apart in absolutely straight rows, and there were 200 square miles of it. We had to go through the Hürtgen to get to the two big dams that controlled the level of the Roer River. The Roer River flows north and then northwest across the plain that leads to the Rhine. As long as the Germans held the dams we could not cross the Roer River because, if we had, the Germans would have isolated us by opening the dams and flooding the plain. It was as simple as that.

"So what happened here?" John Launois, the photographer, says. He was 12 years old and living in Paris at the time, and in each place he tries to get the feeling of it first.

"Everything happened here," George Hicks ways. "It was, I suppose, the closest thing we had to the jungle fighting in the Pacific and, in its own way, it was perhaps as bad."

There is a light rain, and we are sitting in the car in the lane. On the left the wooded ground rises, but on the right it is flat and there are the open, brown-carpeted aisles between the fir trees, with the branches starting about 10 feet above the ground. Beneath the branches and between the trees the still, gray air has that look of twilight even at midday.

We had five infantry divisions and elements of four other units chewed up in here in three months. The Germans had six divisions and parts of two others. There were 120,000 Americans in this forest and 80,000 Germans, and each side had about 33,000 casualties. In World War II, 10 percent casualties was high, and we had more than 25 percent and the Germans more than 40 percent in the Hürtgen.

"The Germans had all the major roads and crossroads zeroed in with artillery," George Hicks is saying, "and pillboxes and bunkers among the trees. Between the trees they had thin, almost invisible trip wires that would set off chains of explosives, and they had four or five different types of mines."

The mine the men feared most was the one called Bouncing Betty. When it was triggered it would come up out of the ground and go off between a man's knees and his groin.

The 9th Division made 3,000 yards here and lost 4,500 killed, wounded and missing, and one regiment lost 2,600 out of 3,200 men, including, within 36 hours, four battalion commanders. The 4th Division had 2,000 casualties for a mile of gain. In 10 days some companies lost as many as four commanders, and it was a good day when they got the replacements into the line without losses. Ernest Hemingway once suggested that it would save everybody a lot of trouble if they just shot them as soon as they got out of the trucks.

"The Germans really fought here," George Hicks is saying.

"Yes," I say, "they took one wounded GI and booby-trapped him so that, if anybody picked him up, the explosive charge would blow him and anybody near him to pieces. He lay in the cold and rain for three days and, when our people got to him, he was still conscious enough to tell them to defuse the charge, and he lived."

"Incredible," John Launois says.

The whole thing was incredible. It rained most of the time and the water ran into the holes, and the men slept in it and got pneumonia and trench foot. Then the first snow came, wet snow and wind-driven, and it fell on the men and into their food and into their coffee, and it plastered their helmets and the sides of the ambulances so that, through it, the red crosses showed pink.

"It was haunting," George Hicks says. "The men were like wraiths appearing and disappearing between the trees."

I spent a whole day watching them pick up dead Americans. The lieutenant was 23 years old and wore silver-rimmed eyeglasses, and he had six men and two jeeps. They lifted them onto the stretchers, and then rolled them off the stretchers into the trailers behind the jeeps. When the trailers were full they pulled the tarpaulins over them. It was raining, and on the ride back the rain ran in rivulets off the tarpaulin, and the men said they didn't mind it so much anymore. They said that at first they were always picking up friends, but now they seldom found anyone they knew. At the collecting point they took them out of the trailers and stacked them between the trees, and the people from Quartermaster would take them from there in the trucks.

"What does this place mean?" John Launois says.

The roads are all two-lane blacktop now, with white stripes down the middle, the roads that were all dirt and then mud with the tanks and the tank destroyers and half-tracks and jeeps stuck in them, and the men up to their knees in the mud trying to get them out. The Germans are out on the roads in their cars now, and along the sides there are the walkers. Well-to-do middle-aged Germans are great walkers in their good rain gear and the men carrying canes.

"They used to call this 'The Million-Dollar Corner,'" I say. "They figured that in three days we expended one million dollars' worth of material here."

"This was all splintered firs," George Hicks says. "There were no farms here then, just broken forest, and the pillbox we tried to get to was off down there in that new wood near the edge of the farm."

"Chick Hennen should see this," I say.

Major Norbert J. Hennen was out of Sheboygan Falls, Wisconsin, and he fascinated me. He was a wry little guy who had been in it since Africa, and he was very tough and he never smiled. On most of our people the American helmet looked like an inverted mixing bowl, but the way he cocked his over one eye it made me think of a snap-brim hat. They were going to burn the Germans out of the pillbox with a flamethrower, but when we got within 100 yards of it the tree bursts started. The air was filled with the splintering noise and the shrapnel and the tops of the trees coming down, and Hennen was sitting on one of the fallen limbs and whistling The Darktown Strutters' Ball. *For months after that I wanted to try to get him drunk to find out what made him like that, but I never saw him again, and now he's a lawyer in Minneapolis.*

"Yes," the forester named Karl Buch is saying, "we still find bodies. American. German. In March, after the snow go, we find seven German. They all time find soldiers."

"Can you usually identify them?" I say.

"All bones, but sometimes material," he says, tugging at the collar of his jacket. "Sometimes helmet. Sometimes *Namenschild.* Name tag."

"Dog tag," I say.

"Yes," he says, smiling. "Dog tag."

He was captured in Africa in 1942 and for two and a half years cut sugarcane and harvested rice in Louisiana and Texas. He is wearing a short green woolen jacket with braided silver epaulets and a golden acorn woven into each epaulet, gray woolen breeches, gray woolen stockings, thick-soled shoes, and there is a tuft of boar hair in the band of his green alpine hat.

"More weapons, though," he says. "Explosives enough to start another war."

He has led us off the road and down the hillside and into the tight little valley of the Kyll River. Along the bank of the river one of the clearing crews has marked the safe path between the trees with white and blue iron stakes, and where the white and red stakes stand beyond the others they have yet to search. In the 20 years they have cleared about half of this forest, and it will take the crews another 20 years to clear it all, and 160 civilians and workers have been killed.

"American issue of *Panzerfaust*," he says, picking up one of our bazooka shells from among the German and American hand grenades in the wooden box. "Very dangerous. Bullets in trees bad for sawmills too."

To the left, along the riverbank, they are working in pairs. There is the humming of the mine detectors, and then the high-pitched singing whine of one of them, and then the sound of a shovel striking the ground once.

"*Namenschild!*" one of them with a shovel is saying, walking up to John Launois and showing it to him. "*Namenschild!*"

It is an American dog tag, with the name and serial number and the years of the tetanus shots and the blood type and the religion. It reads:

CLAUDE M. GARRISON
35475221—T–42–43—AB
P

Later we checked. He was killed in action on November 8, 1944.

"Yes, I like my work," the forester named Buch is saying. "I love the trees, the woods. I am content. I have peace here now."

Vicht, Germany

"Here!" the old waiter is saying to the young waiter who has just come out of the bar. The old waiter is pointing through the window toward the house. "He says the American writer Hemingway lived there."

"That's right?" the young waiter says.

"Yes," I say. "Twenty years ago, during the fighting in the forest, he lived there for perhaps a month."

"I never heard that," the young waiter says. "No one here knows that."

"But you have heard of Hemingway?"

"Oh, yes," the young waiter says. "*Old Man and Sea.*"

It is a two-story, square, fieldstone house on the left of the road about 75 yards from the hotel. On the right, and almost directly across the road, there is another two-story house, but rectangular and red brick, and I remember now that one of the families who lived there had a baby. There was a battery of guns behind the house, and when they fired at night they awakened the baby and it cried.

"She says," the interpreter is saying of the gray-haired woman standing in the hallway and searching our faces, "that she never heard of Hemingway."

"How about her husband?" I say. He is also gray-haired, slim and immaculate, and wearing a gray-checked sports jacket and gray slacks.

"She says he does not hear well and has never heard of Hemingway either, but I have explained. She is happy to have you in the house you remember."

Hemingway had the big brass bed in what is now the living room, and the dining room was across the hall. There is a wooden featherbed and an armoire and a dresser in what was the dining room, but there used to be a round table and some straight-backed chairs and a pot-bellied wood stove. The front was just three miles up the road in the Hürtgen, and when we got back from the front each afternoon we would write our pieces at the round table and send them back with one of the drivers the 30 miles to the press camp and then eat.

"The former owner," the interpreter is saying, "is dead now 15 years. The present owner also owns the lumber mill up the road."

Up in the Hürtgen there was a dead American lying right across one of the trails. The jeeps and the trucks that had used the trail had had to run over him, and he was there for quite some time before someone complained that he was making a bad impression on the replacements who came up the trail, and they got him out. When Bill Walton tried to write it for Time *the censors wouldn't pass it, claiming that it was an isolated incident and not typical, and bad for morale. This made Hemingway irate.*

He was writing then, when he was not helping command the regiment up in the Hürtgen and fathering the rest of us, for *Collier's*, and I don't know if he ever got it into the magazine but he got it into *Across the River and Into the Trees*.

"There are three families living here now," the interpreter is saying. "Eleven persons."

After that all censors held the low position around the house until they were replaced by all psychiatrists. The psychiatrists got in bad when the major who was a psychiatrist dropped in one evening. He was stocky, black-haired and still young, and he was sitting in one of the straight-backed chairs against the wall, and Hemingway was sitting at the table, and they were discussing combat fatigue when the psychiatrist said it. He said that, in his opinion, Hemingway romanticized war.

"What?" Hemingway said, getting up and walking right over to him. "Did you just say I romanticize war?"

Hemingway was wearing a sheepskin vest with the gray skin side out. It made him bulk bigger than ever.

"Well," the major said, and you could see he was trying to get out of it now. "Yes. At least that's my opinion."

"Where?" Hemingway said. "In what that I have written?"

"Well," the major said, "right now I can't . . . "

"Have you read A Farewell to Arms?*" Hemingway said.*

"No," the major said.

"Have you read For Whom the Bell Tolls?*"*

"No."

"Just what have you read that I have written?"

"Well," the major said, "some short stories."

"Have you ever been to the front?"

"No."

"Would you like to go?

"Yes, I would sometime."

"How about tomorrow morning at eight?"

"Well," the major said, "I can't go tomorrow."

"How about the day after tomorrow?"

"I can't go then, either, but I'll let you know when I can go."

"You do that," Hemingway said.

The major left then, and while Hemingway was pacing the floor one of the others told him about a sister whom, he said, a psychiatrist had ruined. The chaplain was there, another major, but big-boned and with a deep voice and from somewhere in the South.

"Have no truck with that psychiatrist, Papa," the chaplain was saying, leaning back in his chair against the wall. "That psychiatrist is courtin' the devil and defyin' the Lord."

"That's right," Hemingway was saying, pacing.

"That psychiatrist is courtin' the devil, Papa," the chaplain kept saying, "and defyin' the Lord."

I never found out whether the psychiatrist ever got to the front, but the next night Hemingway felt a lot better. He was writing a love letter for one of the GI's who stayed at the house. The GI kept getting love letters from his girl back in the small farm town he came from, but he wasn't much of a writer, and Hemingway answered them all. A couple of times he read us passages he particularly liked and, although I never learned how that romance came out, I often thought that someday, perhaps in an attic of a farmhouse somewhere, someone would find tied with a pink ribbon some love letters that would be most unusual.

"Ah, the interpreter is saying, "this man has heard of Hemingway. This man lives upstairs."

He is a small man, thin, with an aquiline face, and he is nodding.

"He says he heard Hemingway's name on TV. He says he knows nothing about him as a writer, but he heard his name and he has asked if Hemingway killed himself."

"What did you tell him?"

"I told him I do not know. Then he said it is not possible that Hemingway would kill himself. When I asked him why he is so sure, he said, 'If a man is well known and has a lot of money, and he is an American, he doesn't kill himself.'"

"Let's thank these people," I am saying. "They've been very kind."

"But I don't understand this man from upstairs," the interpreter is saying. "That makes no sense what he said."

Henri-Chapelle, Belgium

They had the three stakes set in the ground in front of the back wall of the low, gray-stucco munitions building. It was two days before Christmas, and they shot the three German spies at 9:30 in the morning.

"*Mon commandant?*" the *adjudant première classe* is saying into the phone. "*Adjudant première classe* René Parisse, *mon commandant*. There is an American journalist here, *mon commandant*, who witnessed here the execution of the three German spies. Yes, *mon commandant*, I, too, was here, and he is correct. All of the details he tells me are correct. Yes. Thank you, *mon commandant*."

It was during the Bulge, and the Germans were dropping them in American uniforms by parachute and sending others through our lines in American jeeps. Before they shot the three, a young captain briefed us in the big, barnlike room in the red-brick barracks building at the left of the quadrangle. It was as cold in the room as it was outside, but the young captain was very efficient.

"You witnessed the execution?" I am saying to the *adjudant première classe*. He is short and stocky, with blond curly hair and heavy blond eyebrows and pale blue eyes. He walks with a restricted gait because he was wounded in the right leg, as well as the right arm, when the Germans came through Belgium in May of '40.

"Oh, no," he says. "Only Americans were permitted, but I saw the three Germans when they marched them to be shot. I saw that."

The young captain explained that the three had had an American radio transmitter and receiver in the American jeep, but that they never got by the first M.P., who stopped them. He said that the leader was a Nazi, but that the two others were just ordinary soldiers. One of them was a farm boy, and we got the impression that the captain felt the farm boy had been innocent of any intent to spy.

"He's quite simple and, I think, honest," he said. "He says that several weeks before this German counteroffensive started, a call went out for men who spoke English. He thought it would be a soft job back at headquarters in propaganda or prisoner interrogation. The next thing he knew he was in an American uniform and in an American jeep and heading for our lines."

The captain said all three seemed to be taking it well. He said we had some Wehrmacht nurses in the next cell and, the last night, they had been granted permission to sing Christmas carols for the three. He said the only carol he recognized was Silent Night, but then they had had to stop the singing. He said it was unnerving our troops.

"And this is where they marched," the *adjudant première classe* is saying, motioning. "They marched here."

"I know," I say. The munitions building is on the left, and we are walking out into the field where we turned and faced the wall. There are two cows—black-and-white Holsteins—grazing in the field. The field slopes slightly away from the wall, and beyond the barbed-wire fence the ground drops away into the valley. It is a gentle, farming valley, and it widens out to the northwest, and you can see for miles.

So that technically they will not be shot in American uniforms, I was thinking. The three were dressed in GI fatigues, but with a light blue stripe painted down the front of each leg. The farm boy was first, tall and loose-limbed, and then the Nazi, short and with a prominent forehead and steel-rimmed glasses, and then the other. As the farm boy walked across in front of us, he kept looking back, trying to be certain that he was in step with the M.P.'s behind him. When he backed against the stake he was trying, with his whole posture and looking back again, to make it easier for the two M.P.'s who tied first his ankles and then his wrists to the stake.

While they were pinning the white paper disks, the size of a grapefruit, one over the heart of each of the three, I turned and looked at the valley again. There was a mist in the valley, but it was starting to take on a brassy tint from the sun trying to work through it. I could make out three white farm buildings on the valley floor, a little yellowed now in the weak sunlight, and I knew that this would be the last view their eyes would ever see, the last valley, the last room.

"So, look at this," the *adjudant première classe* is saying. We are standing at the wall, the three areas chipped where the bullets hit, and the *adjudant première classe* has pried out a blackened piece of lead. "For you? A souvenir?"

"No," I say, "but thank you."

The Nazi rejected the chaplain who walked up to the stakes, but the two others accepted him. Then they blindfolded them, and the Nazi shouted something about a long life for his Führer *and they died.*

"But see here," the *adjudant première classe* is saying, pointing to the chips out of the overhang two feet above his head. "The Americans did not shoot well. Why?"

"They had never done it before," I say.

Eight M.P.'s fired at each white disk, but even at 20 paces one of the targets had only three bullet holes in it. The cap-

tain said it would have been better if we had used combat troops out of the line.

"This corporal here," John Launois is saying, "says that that is not the only mistake the Americans made here. He doesn't like Americans."

It is not the tall, thin, sandy-haired corporal with the long nose who polices the barracks with the *adjudant pre-mière classe* and whose name is Sameese. This one is shorter, with a finely chiseled face and a strong jaw and dark eyes.

"What's his complaint?" I say.

"You Americans left a lot of babies here," the corporal says. "Not only white babies, but black babies."

"Oh?" John Launois says, and he is pointing across the valley now to where you can just see the flagpole and the American flag. "Do you see that? Look at that. The Americans also left more than 7,900 bodies over there."

"I know," the corporal says.

After they cut the three down, there were just the three white mattress covers, one before each stake and each bulked out by a body, and strewn on the frozen ground were the black-paper ends from the photographers' film packs, the expended flashbulbs, milky-white, and an empty, crumpled Lucky Strike cigarette package. When we got back to the press camp the weather cleared and the Germans came over and bombed us. They killed Jack Frankish of the United Press and three Belgians who were guarding the bridge, and the colonel named Flynn Andrew died later in the hospital.

The three posts are, of course, no longer there. The gray stucco wall, however, is still marked in three places, bullet-pocked. I do not know where the three Germans were buried, but if one stands where they last stood and looks across the valley now, and if the wind and the light are just right, one can see, where the ground rises gently at the far right, an American flag flying. It flies over the cemetery at Henri Chapelle where, their graves marked by the precise rows of crosses and Stars of David, are buried 7,900 Americans.

Chaudfontaine, Belgium

It was such a good hotel that it was embarrassing. It was four stories, rectangular, with a white-brick-and-glass facade, and it faced onto the formal garden. Across the formal garden was the gambling casino. The gambling casino wasn't operating, of course, but it was there with its big picture windows looking out onto the formal garden with the low hedges and the flower beds. The two generals, Montgomery and Bradley, had used the hotel the day before.

"They are Germans," the mayor is saying. His name is William Grisard de la Rochette and he is 79 years old and raises Thoroughbred racehorses, and he was also the mayor 20 years ago. We are standing on the front terrace of the hotel in the late-afternoon sunlight and watching the three buses make the turn around the formal garden and stop in front of the casino. "Half of the clients of the casino now are Germans. They come from Cologne and Düsseldorf."

The colonel who ran the press camp was named Flynn Andrew, and he had said that there would be a briefing in the dining room after lunch, but I had walked out and around the garden instead. They had the jeeps and trailers and trucks parked between the casino and the hill, and I wanted to find the two bottles of champagne. I had been saving them to take them up to some of our people in the line on Christmas Eve, but when I found the trailer and pulled the tarpaulin back and opened my barracks bag they were gone.

The driver was very occupied with his head under the hood of the jeep, but I knew he was a thief anyway. He kept protesting and saying that I had it all wrong, and then I heard the first plane. When I looked up it was right over us and I could see the black crosses on it, and the pilot.

"You will remember," the mayor is saying, "that the first day the correspondents use my château. The colonel was speaking in the great room and the bomb fell and one was wounded, and the colonel was slightly wounded too. Then they say to me: 'This is not good place.' I obtained, then, the hotel, and the next day the colonel is speaking now here and the bombs fall and a correspondent is killed, and the colonel is wounded again and this time dies in the hospital."

When the first one hit I was lying, with the driver who was a thief, under a truck. It hit in front of the hotel and to the right, and the orange bowl of the explosion hid that side of the hotel. Then, next to us, I heard the glass go like the ice breaking up in a frozen waterfall, and lying there on my belly under the truck I could see the GI's at the left of the garden leaping the hedges and running toward the right while those on the right were running toward the left, and they were passing in the middle of the garden.

"It is strange," the mayor is saying, "that you should be bombed one day at my château and then the next day here."

After the first one hit I reasoned that, if there were enough of them, they might try for the motor pool, so I hollered to the driver who was still a thief, and we ran for the casino. The second one hit just as we were stepping in through the window, and then the air was full of plaster dust, and I fell on top of a GI who was lying face down and crying. When I looked out of the window, the whole front of the hotel seemed to be sagging. There was a truck burning off to the left. As I started around the garden and back toward the hotel, the gas tank of the truck exploded, and then one of the tires went.

"I remember you standing right on this step," I am saying to George Hicks. "You had a cut on one cheek and one hand was cut."

"I remember Casey Dempsey," George Hicks says, meaning the captain who ran the press camp for a while and whom we all respected. "We were all wondering who that was, lying out there, and I was trying to crawl over to see. I was actually crawling, but Casey walked right over and bent down and looked at the dog tag and straightened up and said: 'It's Jack Frankish.' God, how I admired the way he did that."

When we pulled out we had to drive by the dead Belgians at the bridge, and a Belgian woman was standing, looking down at one of them, and crying. Just north of Liége a V-1 landed about 75 yards ahead of us and we could see the people on the sidewalk just rise up into the air. They went up into the air and turned over, some with their arms and legs spread out, and came down again. When we got to Maastricht it was dark, and the German planes were looking for the bridges, but we finally found the hotel. There was a lieutenant just inside the door waiting for us with a bottle of Scotch, and a waitress in a black dress with a white apron and wearing a white Dutch cap took our coats. All the waitresses were dressed like that, and at one end of the dining room there was a band in dinner jackets and they were swinging Honeysuckle Rose.

"A man we knew," I am saying to the director of the American cemetery at Henri-Chapelle, "is buried here."

I am standing in the small office at one end of the colonnade. The director is sitting at one desk, and there is a Belgian working at some papers at another.

"If you give me his name," the director says, "I can look up the location of his grave."

"His name . . . " I say, and I stop. The directors of our military cemeteries in Europe say it happens all the time. They say that many Americans who come back cannot go beyond the beginning of the grave areas.

"I'm sorry," I say. "His name was John Frankish and he was a war correspondent and he came from El Centro, California."

"That's all right," the director says. "I'll look it up."

I start to look around the small office, and then I see again the Belgian at the other desk. He has his handkerchief to his face and he has been quietly crying into it.

"Do you have many visitors this time of year?" I am asking the director, whose name is Ambrose Decker. "I mean, after the American tourist season?"

George Hicks and I have walked to the grave and we have walked back. Now we are starting back up the broad steps to the colonnade.

"Oh, yes," the director says. "Just this morning we had six big busloads of Germans."

"Why do you suppose the Germans want to visit our cemeteries?" I say.

"I don't know," the director says. "I've wondered myself, but I can't answer that. They ask a lot of questions too. How many dead? How many unknown?"

"It's on the tour," George Hicks says, "and German tourists will look at anything."

Trois-Ponts, Belgium

The old woman was wearing a gray housedress and slippers and sitting on the front lawn in the rocking chair in the snow. There was a small, blackened bullet hole in the middle of her forehead, and on the four miles of road between Stavelot and Trois-Ponts the S.S. killed 116 other civilians. That, of course, was after they had killed the 146 American prisoners who stood with their hands over their heads in the field at the crossroad south of Malmedy.

"In this house," the woman is saying in English, "all persons were killed but two or three."

The woman is middle-aged now and wearing a gray-checked suit and carrying a black purse. She is standing in front of the row of small houses and it is a Sunday and she has to pause to be heard between the exhaust sounds of the traffic.

"In this other house," she is saying, "a father, mother and two sons and a baby lived. The baby has been killed in its small bed, then the father and the mother. The six- or seven-year-old boy the S.S. shot here in the road. As he ran they shoot him to make fun. They shoot him first in arm and then in leg and finally they killed him. The other boy of eighteen ran away and save his life."

One of the houses is of red brick, another is of field-stone and another of stucco and they are less than 10 feet from the road and the traffic. There is an elderly man looking out of the window of the fieldstone house and studying us.

"In that house," the woman says, being careful not to gesture, "there were 70 persons in the cellar. The S.S. soldier came and said, 'In a few hours you will be killed.' Then the S.S. soldier came again and saw a young woman and said, 'If you make love with me no one will be killed.' The people, see, wanted to be in life. They said nothing and the young woman went with the S.S. soldier to make love with him. Then the S.S. soldier kept his word, because the people were not killed."

"How," I am saying above the noise of the traffic, "do 69 people who owe their lives to her thank a woman like that?"

"By not saying anything," the woman says. "After the war is ended the woman left the town."

Honsfeld, Belgium

The snow was waist high, so there were only a few land-marks to remember. As it was, when the lieutenant in the white snowsuit and the sergeant came in off patrol, the lieutenant located the barn at the wrong coordinates and the stone wall on the wrong side of the road, and the sergeant, always begging his pardon, had to set him straight. The lieutenant had just been in it too long.

"We must have come down from over there," I say, pointing to the right of the road. "We mounted up in a stand of pines on a rise like that. It was 1:15 in the morning."

They had the tanks painted white and, because of the waist-deep snow, the infantry rode the tanks down the 1,500 yards to the edge of the town. It was bright moonlight, with the blue flames spitting out of the tank exhausts and the men bunched behind the turrets, and the first tanks starting to fire into the town, when the 88-mm shell hit. It hit about 25 yards off to the left, the flame and then the snow rising and then the smoke and the black on the snow, and when it hit, the lieutenant facing me made his move. He threw one leg over the side of the tank but, as he did, the sergeant next to him swung his arm across, and he had the lieutenant pinned now against the turret.

"I'm sorry, sir," the sergeant said, holding the lieutenant, "but you'd better not."

"But we'll all get killed," the lieutenant was saying, looking at the sergeant and his voice rising. "We'll all get killed!"

"You'll get killed if you leave this tank, sir," the sergeant said.

"But we'll all get killed!" the lieutenant was saying.

"I'm sorry, sir," the sergeant said.

The sergeant kept his hold on the lieutenant until the tank stopped and we unloaded. It wasn't until sometime later that I realized that the lieutenant and the sergeant on the tank were the same two who had been out on patrol, that the lieutenant was the one who had just been in it too long.

"This is the town all right," I am saying. "It's just that it seems so much smaller."

They all seem so much smaller. There are hundreds of towns like this that the GI's fought for and took and that seemed so much larger then and seem so much smaller now. Only 404 people live in this town.

"He says that he was here then," the interpreter says, meaning the old man in the blue work clothes and with the red face and the halo of hair and the spot of gray paint on the bridge of his nose. "He was in a cellar, but he says you came from the southwest with the tanks, and the snow was waist high."

"That's right," I say. "Ask him if a barn was burning right here at the fork in the road."

"He says yes."

When the call came to unload, the barn was already burning and lighted the snow orange and the tanks orange and the men orange as they jumped off the tanks to start toward the crossroad. Some of them fell on their hands and knees and some of them sat right down and looked pathetic and swore. Then the two lines started, one down on each side of the road, the tanks moving between, the men lighted figures running and slipping in the loose snow, bent over and keeping their intervals and breaking off to take the

houses, dark, on both sides of what had now become a
street. There was the sound of small-arms fire from the
houses and then ahead the brrrp-brrrp of a German burp
gun.

"Machine gunners. Machine gunners," the request came
down the line, distant first and then louder and then passed
on and diminishing behind. "Machine gunners."

The men rested then, many of them on their hands and
knees in the snow, and the machine gunners came up the
road between the two lines. There were the men with the
guns and the men with the tripods over their shoulders,
running and slipping and running and then, after a while,
there was the heavy chut-chut-chut of the machine guns,
and the lines started forward again.

"Medics. Medics. Medics," the word came down the line.
"Medics. Medics. Medics."

The next morning in the command post in the dining
room of the house there was a young second lieutenant who
said he had lost his helmet, and once he picked mine up
from the floor, but I showed him my name on the liner. I
did not see him go out, but later mine was missing, and
when we went back past the fork in the road the young sec-
ond lieutenant was directing traffic there and he was wear-
ing a helmet.

"How did it go?" the captain named Max Zera, who was
the PRO of the 1st Infantry Division, was asking me a cou-
ple of nights later at the press camp.

I said it went fine, but then I told him about the young
second lieutenant and the helmet. I said I saw him wear-
ing a helmet at the fork in the road and that I bet it was
mine.

"What time did you see him?" Max said.

"Oh," I said, "about 11:15."

"You'll never cash your bet," Max said. "Just before noon
a shell came in and took his head off."

Remagen, Germany

It was the only bridge still standing on the Rhine, and when the first Americans started across it they knew it was wired for demolition. They knew that at any moment the whole bridge could go and take them with it, and they had to run 1,000 feet, 700 of them over water. It was one of the bravest acts of the war.

"Can you imagine what a run that was?" I say.

We are standing at the two blackened brownstone towers on the west bank and looking across at the two oval brownstone piers in the river, the wild grass, brown now, sticking out of the tops of them, and at the two towers on the other side. That is all that is left now, but there are the Rhine River barges passing, black with white trim and, on one of them, the laundry hanging on the deck in the sunlight, and a white excursion steamer from Holland.

"It scares the hell out of you," John Launois says, "just to stand here and think of it."

It ended after Remagen, after the 9th Armored Division captured the only bridge on the Rhine. There were still two months of it, and some of the fighting was vicious and many died, but then it was the tanks rolling again as they had rolled, after the breakthrough, through France and Belgium.

"All right," he says in English, sitting down at one of the tables in the small, plain bar-and-dining-room. "I am busy, but I give you five minutes. What you want to know?"

His name is Gerhard Rothe, and he is 52 now, and he has become a local celebrity. He inherited from his father the 40-bed hotel across the plaza from the railroad station, but he inherited his fame when he was the last German soldier to retreat across the Remagen Bridge.

After the bridge, even the German High Command knew it was over, and they executed three majors and a first lieutenant. After our tanks it was our infantry riding in the trucks and the white bedsheets of surrender hanging out of the windows of the German towns. Then it was the trucks rolling back through the towns, this time filled with the prisoners standing 70 packed in a truck.

"Ach!" he says. "That story I tell too many times."

He is tired of our war. Sitting here in this small bar of his own hotel, wearing a white smock and looking like a grocery-store owner, tall, lean, wearing glasses, his black hair streaked with gray, he would rather be doing something else.

It was clever the way they got 70 prisoners into each truck. They faced them standing forward and, when a truck was full, the prisoners packed so tightly that it was impossible to add the five or six more, the M.P. would shout to the driver. The driver would start the truck and go about 20 feet and suddenly stop. As the prisoners shifted forward, the M.P. would add the others to make the 70 in each truck and then put up the tailgate.

"So I am first sergeant and come down from the hill with my group," he says, "and on the road to Coblenz there is armored car and a machine gun fires and I am wounded in legs. So I have to crawl across the bridge, and I am the last one."

As the trucks rolled through the small towns, it was the women throwing the bread to the prisoners. The bread would bounce off the sides of the trucks and out of the prisoners' hands and roll in the dust and be crushed by the trucks. Some of the women cried, and a few of them held up babies.

"So when you were taken prisoner," I ask him, "the Americans treated you well?"

"The first thing they have done is take my watch away," he says. "It was good watch."

Before the bridge collapsed on the 10th day, the Germans tried to knock it out with everything they had left. They put planes on it and artillery, rockets, frogmen and floating mines. Along both sides of the river we had the largest concentration of anti-aircraft put together in Europe, and it was a show the day they got 16 out of 21 planes, and I saw the baby.

"Tell her," I am saying to the interpreter, and we have crossed on the car ferry to Linz and come up the east bank to just south of where the bridge used to be, "that I met her last when her daughter was three days old."

"He was there?" the woman says surprised, and we are sitting in the small living room of the gray-stucco house. "He remembers where that other house was?"

The 40-mm ack-ack gun with the sandbags around it was in the front yard of the white-stucco house against the hill. The two GI's had come running up to the medic's station to say a baby was being born right behind their gun. The captain named Albert J. Haft, from Queens, New York, had gone back with them and into the cellar. In the light of two flashlights, and with the German planes making three runs at the bridge and the sound and the vibrations coming into the cellar, he had delivered the baby.

"He remembers," the woman says, nodding. She is 42 now and in her blond hair there is gray. She has three children now.

"Tell her," I say, "that in the cellar she and the baby were lying in a big wooden bed under a red quilt. There was a table and a kitchen sink and a kerosene lamp, and a gray-haired woman was taking care of her and the baby."

"He is right," she says, nodding. "He remembers."

"Tell her," I say, "that I have been looking forward to seeing her daughter again, and talking with her."

"Oh," the interpreter says, and I have it already. "The girl is not alive."

"I'm sorry," I say, because I can think of nothing else to say. "I'm very sorry."

"The baby lived only seven days," the interpreter is saying. "She says there was something wrong. The baby slept all the time. She was never really alive."

"I'm sorry," I say. "Tell her I'm sorry I came."

"She says she is glad you came. She says she is happy to see someone who remembers her baby."

I am still sorry I came. I had wanted, at the end of it, at the end of all the seeking, to find not whatever there was but whatever there is. I had wanted to find the 19-year-old, blue-eyed, blond German girl. I remember how she was born, and that was in my world and in my time, but now my own youth is gone and I am middle-aged. I had wanted her to talk to me of her world, of what she does and what she thinks and what she dreams. I had wanted to find what came out of my world for hers, but that was impossible, of course. It was impossible, for the 19-year-old, blue-eyed, blond German girl never really was.

"She asks now," the interpreter says, "if you will have a glass of wine."

"Tell her I thank her," I say, "but tell her we have to make a train and that I am going home."